THE SPIRIT OF
PHILADELPHIA

THE SPIRIT OF PHILADELPHIA

PHILADELPHIA

Social Justice vs. the Total Market

ALAIN SUPIOT

Translated by Saskia Brown

V

VERSO

London • New York

Liberté • Égalité • Fraternité
RÉPUBLIQUE FRANÇAISE

This book is supported by the Institut français as part of the Burgess programme
(www.frenchbooknews.com)

This English-language edition first published by Verso 2012
© Verso 2012
Translation © Saskia Brown
First published as *L'esprit de Philadelphie: La justice sociale face au marché total*
© Seuil 2010

1 3 5 7 9 10 8 6 4 2

Verso
UK: 6 Meard Street, London W1F 0EG
US: 20 Jay Street, Suite 1010, Brooklyn, NY 11201
www.versobooks.com

Verso is the imprint of New Left Books

ISBN-13: 978-1-84467-754-2

British Library Cataloguing in Publication Data
A catalogue record for this book is available from the British Library

Library of Congress Cataloging-in-Publication Data

Supiot, Alain.
 [Esprit de Philadelphie. English]
 The spirit of Philadelphia : social justice against the
total market / Alain Supiot ; translated by Saskia
Brown.
   p. cm.
 ISBN 978-1-84467-754-2
1. Liberalism--Social aspects. 2. Globalization--
Social aspects. 3. Social justice. I. Title.
 HB95.S8613 2012
 303.3'72--dc23

                                                    2012002826

Typeset in Sabon by Hewer Text UK Ltd, Edinburgh
Printed in the US by Maple Vail

In memory of Bruno Trentin

CONTENTS

INTRODUCTION

Philadelphia, USA. This was where the very first International Declaration of Universal Rights was born, on 10 May 1944. The Declaration was the first expression of the resolve, as Allied troops advanced across Normandy and the Second World War drew to a close, to found a new international order based not on force but on justice and law. Under the modest title of 'Declaration Concerning the Aims and Purposes of the International Labour Organisation' (ILO), it set out 'the principles which are fully applicable to all peoples everywhere . . . and which should inspire the policy of its Members'. A few weeks later, the Bretton Woods Agreement was signed, and the following year saw the founding of the United Nations, which proclaimed the Universal Declaration of Human Rights in 1948. On several accounts, then, the Declaration of Philadelphia (DePh) was a groundbreaking text, committed to making social justice one of the core principles of any international legal order, and its spirit can be felt in each of the official texts which followed.

On rereading this Declaration, one cannot but be struck by how radically its principles differ from the neo-liberal dogmas which have dominated national and international policy for the last three decades. The propaganda which makes the way economic globalisation has developed appear to be some sort of fact of nature to which the whole of humanity must unquestioningly bow seems to have left intact not even the memory of the lessons learnt from the world wars. The wish to ensure at least a modicum of justice in the production and distribution of wealth globally has been replaced by belief in the infallibility of the financial markets, thereby condemning the countless victims of this new economic world order to migration, social exclusion and violence. The present collapse of the system is an opportunity to bring to light, from under the rubble of its neo-liberal ideology, the normative instruments elaborated at the end of the Second World War, which this ideology precisely busied itself destroying.

The principles laid down at Philadelphia developed out of a harrowing historical experience, which we must reconstruct in order to understand their true significance.[1] In 1944, the world had not yet witnessed the bombing of Hiroshima, the scale of the Shoah was unknown, and Stalin's senseless slaughter was generally denied, and at all events could not be mentioned between the Allies. But Allied victory was already assured. And the Declaration of Philadelphia aimed at laying the foundations for a new world order based on what the 'Thirty Years' War', which had ravaged the world from 1914 to 1945, could teach us. The horrors of this period of unparalleled atrocities, from Verdun to Hiroshima via Auschwitz and the gulag, were not everywhere the same. But these horrors were variations on a single theme: man considered 'scientifically', as 'human material' (Nazi terminology) or 'human capital' (Communist terminology), subjected to the same calculations of utility and the same industrial methods as those used to exploit natural resources.

---

1 On the circumstances in which it was adopted, see E. Lee, 'La Déclaration de Philadelphie: rétrospective et prospective', *International Labour Review* 133: 4, 1994, 467–84.

Previous centuries had, of course, already witnessed how human beings could be regarded as no more than insects, when America was discovered or Africa explored. Until the twentieth century, it was 'primitives' who were treated as things to be exploited or exterminated according to whether they were deemed useful or harmful. The exploitation of the European working classes, on the other hand, was guided by principles of equality and freedom of contract which, far from denying their humanity, were supposed to bring it to fruition. These working classes nevertheless experienced at first hand enslavement to mechanised industry and the industrial management of human resources, which thrust the 'social question' to the forefront of nineteenth-century concerns.

What was new about the horrors of the first half of the twentieth century had its roots in two previously distinct phenomena which fused into one: not only 'primitives' but 'civilised' populations as well were now to be considered and treated as things, and the industrial management of human beings was no longer restricted to the factory, but now became a general principle of government, in peacetime as in war. Scientism brought this synthesis about, since it claimed to base the government of men on laws immanent to nature and society alike. Real scientists are aware that the laws discovered by the natural sciences are inherent in the phenomena observed, whereas those which organise and give meaning to human life are necessarily postulates. But scientism considers science fetishistically, claiming to find within it the 'true laws' governing, and to be applied to, human beings.

The twentieth century was marked by two variants of scientism. One adopted biological and anthropological laws, the other economic and historical ones. While attempts to combine the two[2] have come up

---

2   The idea of grounding the supposed laws of the economy in biology

against their many and far-reaching differences, which should not be underestimated, they yet converge in assigning the government of men not to an ideal of justice but to the play of 'blind forces' conceived as ruling humankind. In Engels' words:

> Socialism became a science. The next thing was to work out all its details and relations . . . The final causes of all social changes and political revolutions are to be sought, not in men's brains, not in men's better insights into eternal truth and justice, but in changes in the modes of production and exchange. They are to be sought, not in the philosophy, but in the economics of each particular epoch . . . Active social forces work exactly like natural forces: blindly, forcibly, destructively, so long as we do not understand, and reckon with, them. But, when once we understand them, when once we grasp their action, their direction, their effects, it depends only upon ourselves to subject them more and more to our own will, and, by means of them, to reach our own ends.[3]

Scientism's normative constructs included eugenics and racial laws (the biologistic version), and dictatorship of the proletariat and 'socialist legality' (the 'scientific socialism' version). However divergent these variants may be, they converge in the belief that the

dates back to the nineteenth century and periodically makes a comeback. The neurosciences today compete with genetics for the attention of economists keen to base the market on the laws of nature. See G.S. Becker, 'Altruism, Egoism, and Genetic Fitness: Economics and Sociobiology', in *The Economic Approach to Human Behavior*, Chicago: University of Chicago Press, 1976, 282ff.; A. Rustichini (ed.), 'Special Issue on Neuroeconomics', *Games and Economic Behavior* 52: 2, Aug. 2005, 201–494.

3 F. Engels, 'Socialism: Utopian and Scientific' (1880), *Marx/Engels: Selected Works*, Moscow: Progress Publishers, 1970, vol. 3, 95–151.

'true laws' of science should apply the world over and that every legal system must bow to them. Scientistic belief, in its subordination of legal systems to some super-human law, clearly mirrors religious belief; faith in the laws *discovered* by Science simply replaces faith in the laws *revealed* by God. One need only pay a visit to the mausoleum in which Lenin's embalmed body awaits resurrection through scientific progress[4] to realise how deeply indebted to Christianity the major twentieth-century ideologies are.

However, we should not neglect the difference between scientistic and religious normative constructs. Even the most deterministic of the religions of the Book (such as Calvinism) allows for free will, whereas in a scientistic universe man is wholly determined by his biological or socio-economic identity. Such 'realism' contests the legitimacy of any and every moral, legal or religious rule, and bids us subject ourselves, and others, to the 'inherent laws' that supposedly govern human life. As Hitler put it,

> Riches, by virtue of an inherent law, belong to him who conquers them . . . That's in accordance with the laws of nature . . . The law of selection justifies this incessant struggle, by allowing the survival of the fittest. Christianity is a rebellion against natural law, a protest against nature. Taken to its logical extreme, Christianity would mean the systematic cultivation of the human failure.[5]

If we believe in these laws without a Legislator, we are enlisted not to convert people but to 'abolish the parasitic

4 See R. Tartarin, 'Transfusion sanguine et immortalité chez Alexandre Bogdanov', in A. Supiot (ed.), *Tisser le lien social*, Paris: Éd. MSH, 2004, 305ff.

5 A. Hitler, *Secret Conversations 1941–1944*, trans. Norman Cameron and R.H. Stevens, New York: Enigma Books, 2008, 41.

sections of society',[6] to destroy those sentenced by the tribunals of history or of race. Destined for the 'rubbish heap of history', as Trotsky put it, 'human refuse' is to be industrially processed by a mixture of forced labour and extermination. This is doubtless the specific signature of the insane massacres which have marked the history of the twentieth century.

The motto of the 1933 Chicago World Fair – 'Science Finds, Industry Applies, Man Conforms' – should alone remind us that the ideology of the scientific processing of human beings was not restricted to totalitarian regimes. The classification of humankind into 'races' organised hierarchically according to their degree of adaptability or civilisation was the dark side of the Enlightenment.[7] Biologistic doctrines and racial anthropology were widespread in the 1930s and, with the notable exception of the United Kingdom (where Parliament refused to succumb to scientistic propaganda), all Protestant countries adopted some eugenic legislation.[8] The fact that the Second World War ended with testing atomic bombs on the civilian inhabitants of Hiroshima and Nagasaki forces us to recognise that democratic regimes can also carry out the industrial liquidation of whole populations. In the words of Leó Szilárd (one of the physicists who had helped develop the atomic bomb, and thereafter attempted to stop it being used): 'if the Germans, rather than us, had dropped atomic bombs, we would have defined the dropping of atomic bombs on cities as a war crime,

6   Declaration of Rights of the Working and Exploited People, drafted under Lenin's supervision and approved by the All-Russia Congress of Soviets on 25 January 1918.

7   A. Pichot, *Aux origines des théories raciales. De la Bible à Darwin*, Paris: Flammarion, 2008.

8   P. Zylberman, 'Les damnés de la démocratie puritaine: stérilisations en Scandinavie, 1929–1977', *Le Mouvement social* 187, 1999, 99–125; A. Pichot, *The Pure Society: From Darwin to Hitler*, trans. David Fernbach, London and New York: Verso, 2009.

sentenced the Germans responsible to death at the Nuremburg Trials and hung them'.[9]

In the eyes of those who seek to subject man to the 'true laws' revealed by God or discovered by Science, a legal system is nothing but a façade lacking any inherent legitimacy. The most radical way to implement this belief has been to abolish the legal system altogether, as the Maoists did during the Cultural Revolution or the Taliban did in Afghanistan. More frequently, a semblance of legality is preserved, but one which can always be overturned by appeal to 'true laws'. In such cases, as Martin Broszat observes concerning the Nazi state, 'The progressive undermining of the principle of law through measures cast in legal form finally resulted in an utterly crude, lawless, criminal action.'[10]

As Harold Berman neatly puts it,[11] socialist legality did not instate the *rule of law* but, at its best (after the death of Stalin), *rule by law*. The rule of law under Communism, as in the Third Reich, was always threatened by overriding discretionary powers, since the law should never be an obstacle to the construction of socialism. 'Socialist legality', in contrast to 'bourgeois legality', did not guarantee the rights of individuals. The first clause of the USSR's Civil Code is unambiguous on this point: 'The law guarantees the rights of citizens, except in cases where exercising them would contradict state-socialist goals.' The Soviet regime is therefore not really based on a shared normative framework (a *régime de Droit*) in the sense of the 1948 Universal Declaration, unless every system of rules can be deemed a legal system. The rules which patients in

9   L. Szilárd, 'President Truman Did Not Understand', *U.S. News & World Report*, 15 Aug. 1960.

10   M. Broszat, *The Hitler State: The Foundation and Development of the Internal Structure of the Third Reich*, London: Longman, 1981, 323.

11   H. Berman, *Law and Revolution*, Cambridge, Mass.: Harvard University Press, 2003, vol. 2, 19.

psychiatric hospitals must observe, for instance, may well form a coherent whole, but that does not make them similar to a legal system, because they can be waived at any moment at the doctor's discretion. They are simply techniques for establishing and standardising a practice derived from the science of medicine. No individual rights are created for the patients interned. In this respect, the term 'purge', routinely and prudishly used to designate Stalin's colossal carnage, is not simply a convenient euphemism to avoid calling by its real name the mass extermination of 'socially harmful elements and people of the past'.[12] Just like 'justice in white coats' (dissidents assimilated to the mentally ill) or 'slimming down the workforce' (sacked employees assimilated to excess weight), 'purge' implies taking a biological state as a norm and, in a move typical of scientism, closing the gap between 'being' and 'ought-to-be', between normality and legality. Such a conflation is unavoidable whenever human society is treated as a thing, a vast organism that functions according to its own internal laws. An organism is never delinquent; it has at most ill or parasitic parts, which should be treated or amputated.

For Nazism, 'law is a human invention. Nature knows neither the notary nor the surveyor. God knows only force.'[13] As for the state, it is 'only the means to an end; the end is the preservation of a community of biologically and spiritually similar beings'.[14] Putting this purely instrumental conception of the state into practice turned the Third Reich into a 'Dual State', one in

---

12 See N. Woerth, 'Les crimes de masse sous Staline (1930–1953)', *Online Encyclopedia of Mass Violence*, 2008: http://www.massviolence.org/Article?id_article=124.

13 A. Hitler, '17 October 1941, evening', in *Secret Conversations*, 54–6.

14 Hitler, *Mein Kampf*. Cit. Ernst Fraenkel, *The Dual State: A Contribution to the Theory of Dictatorship*, Oxford: Oxford University Press, 1941 (repr. Clark, NJ: Lawbook Exchange, Ltd., 2006), 136.

which the state governed by the rule of law was constantly shadowed by the limitless discretionary powers of the prerogative state.[15] Göring's hedonistic version was *Recht ist das, was uns gefällt* ('Law is whatever it pleases us to dispose').[16] Instead of simply obeying laws as laid down, the 'healthy' citizen's duty was to examine and even pre-empt the will of the Führer, who set the goals to be attained rather than the rules to be observed.[17] The National Socialist regime's only 'constitution' was martial law (by a decree of 28 February 1933, which suspended the fundamental rights guaranteed by the Weimar Constitution). This transformed the state of exception into the very foundation of the legal system, as expounded by the most brilliant of the Nazi legal theorists, Carl Schmitt. These sorts of theories result in a disregard for whether political power is bound by a founding norm or not, hence tarring with the same legal brush the totalitarian state and the state governed by the rule of law.

This distinction, which is once again under attack from certain legal theorists who consider it 'non-scientific' and contrary to the neutrality of the legal form, seemed beyond question at the end of the Second World War. History had just demonstrated that the totalitarian state is to the rule of law what madness is to reason – a fantasy of limitless power, which feeds on murder. A new civilised international order clearly had to ensure that all countries acknowledged universally recognised rights and freedoms, and had to lay the normative

---

15 A particularly exemplary expression of this dualism can be found in the secret decree of 7 October 1939 by which Hitler authorised Himmler to 'eliminate the harmful influences of such alien parts of the population as constitute a danger to the Reich and the German community' (cit. M. Broszat, *The Hitler State*, 319).

16 Cit. R. Rhees, in *Discussions of Wittgenstein*, London: Routledge, 1996.

17 See W. Ebenstein, *The Nazi State*, New York: Farrar & Rinehart, 1943, 3ff.

foundations for an ideal of justice shared by 'all peoples and all nations'. Competition between countries was to give way to cooperation, guided not by the particular but by the general interest. The Declaration of Philadelphia and the texts adopted in its wake all sought to subordinate might to right and to elaborate the principles which all legal systems should share. That is why the rule of law was evoked in the 1948 Universal Declaration as an essential condition 'if man is not to be compelled to have recourse, as a last resort, to rebellion against tyranny and oppression'. In the French version of the Declaration, the notion of 'rule of law' was translated by *régime de Droit*, the shared normative framework, rather than the more usual *état de droit*, a choice which aptly reflected the desire to get beyond national differences and found an international legal regime which would not forget the lessons of totalitarianism.

The city of Philadelphia, which had been the centre of the American Enlightenment in the eighteenth century, could not have provided a better symbol for this enterprise. Its name derives from the Greek ΦιλαδέλΦια ('brotherly love'), emblematising the desire of its founders in 1681 for a world of brotherhood and religious tolerance. President Franklin Roosevelt was a worthy heir to this enlightened aspect of the American tradition when he evoked the four freedoms which should reign throughout the world, in his famous speech of 6 January 1941: 'freedom of speech, freedom of religion, freedom from want, freedom from fear'. The last two were the most innovative, particularly the goal of 'freedom from want'. This idea, inspired by Keynes and the experience of the New Deal, linked social justice inextricably to economic prosperity, where 'want' had the sense both of man's *needs* and of *demand* on the markets. It was taken up again in Roosevelt and Churchill's Atlantic Charter of August 1941, which lay the foundations for post-war international policy, aiming at 'bringing about the fullest collaboration between all nations in the economic field with the object of securing, for all, improved labor standards, economic advancement and social security'. These political statements strongly influenced the legal innovations at the end of the war, which were in the same spirit. This 'spirit of Philadelphia' is characterised by five fundamental elements, which can be found not only in the eponymous Declaration (and which were integrated subsequently into the constitution of the ILO), but also in the Preamble to the Charter of the United Nations, and the Universal Declaration of Human Rights.

Some brief explanatory remarks are necessary here. These fundamental principles are neither *revealed* by a sacred text nor *discovered* through observing nature, but are *affirmed* by man: 'The Conference reaffirms the fundamental principles . . .' (DePh). This affirmation is *explicitly dogmatic*, expressed in the form of an act of faith: 'We the peoples of the United Nations determined to . . . reaffirm faith in . . .' (UN Ch). Final authority is not vested in God (as in the 1776 American Declaration of Independence or the 1789 French Declaration of the Rights of Man and of the Citizen), nor in Science (as was the case with Nazism and Communism).

Secondly, this act of faith is also an act of reason, since it is based on *experience*. The 'scourge of war, which twice in our lifetime has brought untold sorrow to mankind' (UN Ch), and has 'resulted in barbarous acts which have outraged the conscience of mankind' (UDHR), has 'fully demonstrated the truth of the statement in the Constitution of the International Labour Organisation that lasting peace can be established only if it is based on social justice' (DePh). The instrument which allows people of all nations and all creeds to construct a just system together and to learn from such barbarity is law. That is why 'it is essential, if man is not to be compelled to have recourse, as a last resort, to rebellion against tyranny and oppression, that human rights should be protected by the rule of law [*régime de Droit*]' (UDHR).

Thirdly, in the light of the lethal consequences of reifying the human being, we must recognise that '*the inherent dignity ... of all members of the human family* is the foundation of freedom, justice and peace in the world' (UDHR). Compared to some of the rights and principles declared already before the Second World War, the new element of the equal dignity of 'all human beings, irrespective of race, creed or sex' (DePh) was truly groundbreaking, since it made human dignity into the *founding principle* of any legal system, underlying all rights and fundamental principles. Whereas the latter, such as freedom and equality, have to be weighed up against each other, human dignity is a principle on which no compromise is possible without bringing the whole legal order into jeopardy. This principle, as a response to the experience of human reification, obliges us to view people not only as spiritual but also as physical beings. In their organic make-up and physical needs, people are the same as animals, but they should never be treated as such, in the name of their inherent human dignity. This holistic view of the human being transcended the old opposition between spirit and matter, *psyché* and *soma*, and marked a break both with ideologies that reduce people to human material or capital and with those which, incarnated in previous declarations of human rights, view people as disincarnate rational beings.

The principle of dignity additionally implied *linking the imperatives of freedom and of security*. Human beings are able to exercise their 'freedom of speech and belief' and to be free from 'tyranny and oppression' (UDHR) only if they have sufficient material security and 'economic security' (DePh). The legal system must

therefore contribute to 'promot[ing] ... better standards of life in larger freedom' (UN Ch). The bond
established between security and freedom was what
the four fundamental principles expressed by the
Declaration of Philadelphia had in common: (a) respect
for labour ('labour is not a commodity'), (b) collective
freedoms ('freedom of expression and of association
are essential to sustained progress'), (c) solidarity
('poverty anywhere constitutes a danger to prosperity
everywhere'), and (d) social democracy ('the war
against want requires to be carried on with unrelenting
vigour within each nation, and by continuous and concerted international effort in which the representatives
of workers and employers, enjoying equal status with
those of Governments, join with them in free discussion and democratic decision with a view to the
promotion of the common welfare'). Human dignity
thus implied challenging at once the systems which
flout the need for security in the name of freedom and
those which stifle freedoms in the name of security.

Lastly, the link established between spiritual
freedoms and material security implied that the economy must be organised according to the principle of
social justice. The Constitution of the ILO (1919) had
already declared that 'lasting peace can be established
only if it is based on social justice', but it did not define
the latter, nor did it draw out the implications of this
principle for the economy or for finance. This was
where the Declaration of Philadelphia brought something new. It gave a universal and inclusive definition
of social justice: 'all human beings, irrespective of race,
creed or sex, have the right to pursue both their material well-being and their spiritual development in
conditions of freedom and dignity, of economic security and equal opportunity' (DePh, art. IIa). And social
justice, as defined in the Declaration, should be 'the
central aim of national and international policy'.
Consequently, 'all national and international policies

and measures, in particular those of an economic and financial character, should be judged in this light and accepted only in so far as they may be held to promote and not to hinder the achievement of this fundamental objective' (DePh, art. IIc). In the Philadelphia Declaration, therefore, the economic and financial realms are explicitly *means* to man's ends.

Today's process of globalisation is guided by quite the opposite goals. The goal of social justice has been replaced by that of the free circulation of goods and capital, and the hierarchy of ends and means has been inverted. Roosevelt's four freedoms have given way to the free circulation of goods and capital, and unlimited competition. Instead of indexing the economy to human needs, and finance to the needs of the economy, the economy obeys the demands of finance and human beings are treated as 'human capital' at the disposal of the economy.

The present book sets out to analyse this betrayal, which seems to have eradicated the commitments to social justice born of the period 1914–1945. But it also seeks to show how their spirit has lost nothing of its power for all those who, today, have not abandoned the ideal of a world in which 'all human beings, irrespective of race, creed or sex, have the right to pursue both their material well-being and their spiritual development in conditions of freedom and dignity, of economic security and equal opportunity' (DePh, art. IIa).

PART I

Social Justice Betrayed

1

THE HOLY UNION OF COMMUNISM AND CAPITALISM

As we have seen, the 'spirit of Philadelphia' has today been usurped by its exact opposite, in a volte-face which has two principal causes: the Anglo-American neo-liberal counterrevolution, and the conversion of communist countries to the market economy.

THE NEO-LIBERAL COUNTERREVOLUTION

The 'neo-liberal counterrevolution' was, broadly speaking, the outcome of the radical doctrines applied by the Reagan and Thatcher governments and their successors. Like the French nineteenth-century ultra-royalists, these leaders sought to re-establish a mythical *ancien régime* and erase any trace of the new regime which had succeeded it. Neo-liberalism swept through both the economy and international politics. In the form of economic neo-liberalism (as it is known in continental Europe), it aimed at dismantling the welfare state and restoring the 'spontaneous order of the market'. In its political guise, it took the form of neo-conservatism in international relations, that is, a messianic vision intent on imposing its doctrines on the whole world, if need be by force.

These developments can rightly be called a 'revolution', in the precise sense this term has acquired in the

history of legal systems and institutions.[1] The neo-
liberal doctrines initially applied in the United States
and the United Kingdom in the 1980s, before spread-
ing to all Western countries, had the welfare reforms of
the post-war years as their first target. In the words of
Denis Kessler, one of this counterrevolution's most
eloquent advocates in France, 'the Programme of the
National Council of the Resistance [must] be methodically dismantled'.[2] This Programme, adopted in secret
two months before the Declaration of Philadelphia and
imbued with a similar spirit, contained the outline of a
'social republic', which would later be integrated into
the Preamble to the French Constitution of 1946 (still
in force today). In particular, this Programme made
provision for

> the establishment of the broadest possible democ-
> racy ... freedom of the press and its independence
> from the forces of money ... the creation of a genuine
> social and economic democracy, which means wrest-
> ing economic decision-making from the grip of the
> great economic and financial empires ... the right to
> work and the right to rest, particularly by reestablish-
> ing and improving negotiated labour conditions ...
> reinvesting the trade union movement with its inde-
> pendence and traditional freedoms, and with extensive
> powers in the organisation of social and economic

---

1   See H. Berman, *Law and Revolution*, 2 vols., Cambridge, Mass.:
Harvard University Press, 1983 and 2003.
2   D. Kessler, 'Farewell 1945, Let's Hook Our Country Up to the
World Again!', *Challenges*, 4 Oct. 2007. Kessler, a former communist
sympathiser, became a professor of economics and later the executive
vice president of the MEDEF (*Mouvement des entreprises de France*,
representing business interests), from 1998 to 2002. Today he sits on the
boards of a large number of big businesses (BNP Paribas, Dexia, Bolloré,
Dassault Aviation and INVESCO) and is also a member of powerful
public bodies in France (including the Economic and Social Council, the
Council on National Accounts, and the National Council on Insurance).

life . . . a complete social security scheme, managed jointly by representatives of the parties concerned and the State, to ensure that all citizens have means of existence in all cases in which they are unable to provide for themselves through work.

The call to 'methodically dismantle' the projects for social justice bequeathed by the Resistance should come as no surprise to us in the light of the much more general criticism which the advocates of neo-liberalism have levelled for the last thirty years at all the texts imbued with the spirit of Philadelphia. The most insistent critic has been Friedrich Hayek, one of the fathers of today's economic fundamentalism. Hayek, who received one of the first Nobel Prizes in Economics in 1974, was a lawyer by training. His work was partly devoted to spelling out the legal and institutional reforms called for by his economic doctrines. He maintained that the economic and social rights enshrined in the 1948 Universal Declaration 'could not be enforced by law without at the same time destroying that liberal order at which the old civil rights aim'.[3] Harshly critical of the normative corpus developed at the end of the Second World War,[4] Hayek particularly lambasted its 'unlimited democracy', which extended to economic issues: 'Once we give licence to the politicians to interfere in the spontaneous order of the market . . . they initiate that cumulative process which by inner necessity leads . . . to

---

3 See F.A. Hayek, *Law, Legislation and Liberty: A New Statement of the Liberal Principles of Justice and Political Economy*, vol. 2: *The Mirage of Social Justice*, Chicago: University of Chicago Press, 1976, 103.

4 'The whole document', says Hayek, referring to the 1948 Universal Declaration, 'is indeed couched in that jargon of organizational thinking which one has learnt to expect in the pronouncements of trade union officials or the International Labour Organization . . .; this jargon is altogether inconsistent with the principles on which the order of a Great Society rests.' Ibid., 105.

an ever-growing domination over the economic process by politics.'[5] This criticism determined the primary objective of the neo-liberal revolution, namely to insulate the 'spontaneous order' of the market from the ballot box. The political sphere, in this doctrine, should have no say in the distribution of work and resources, nor in the workings of the financial sector. This restriction of democracy was deemed necessary in order to prevent ignorant people from meddling with the laws of the economy, which are way beyond them: 'To them the market economy is largely incomprehensible; they have never practised the rules on which it rests, and its results seem to them irrational and immoral . . . Their demand for a just distribution in which organized power is to be used to allocate to each what he deserves, is thus strictly an *atavism*, based on primordial emotions.'[6]

Since, for Hayek, all the institutions based on the principle of solidarity derive from an 'atavistic idea of distributive justice', they will inevitably wreck the 'spontaneous order of the market', which is based on the truth of the price mechanism and the pursuit of individual gain. Dismantling such institutions therefore logically accompanied the restriction of democracy. And the neo-liberal programme aimed not only at 'dismantling' these, but also at preventing them from ever recovering. That is why it was necessary to 'dethrone politics' using constitutional measures, such that 'all use of coercion to assure a certain income to particular groups (beyond a flat minimum for all who cannot earn more in the market) [should] be outlawed as immoral and strictly antisocial'[7].

---

5   F.A. Hayek, op. cit., vol. 3: *The Political Order of a Free People*, Chicago: University of Chicago Press, 1979, 151. On this aspect of Hayek's theory, see P. Anderson, *The New Old World*, London: Verso, 2009, 64–7.

6   Ibid., 165.

7   Ibid., 150. And see also chap. 18, 'The Containment of Power and the Dethronement of Politics', 128–52.

The resolve to depoliticise the economic field also affected economists, who mostly deserted the learned tradition of 'political economy' for an 'economic science' which aped the hard sciences. This 'science' even managed to place under the aegis of Alfred Nobel the prizes by which it congratulated itself on its own supposed achievements.[8] The aspiration to the legitimacy of a science emerged at the same time as the neo-liberal revolution and was one of its essential components. Since, in a democratic society, only scientific and religious norms may be placed beyond political scrutiny, believing – and making others believe – that economic systems are scientific is part and parcel of the project of depoliticisation. The neo-liberal revolution thus unwittingly revived the grand tradition of scientism, and particularly the ideology of scientific socialism, with its faith in the existence of immanent economic laws which the political realm is supposed to implement without argument.

Not only does neo-liberal doctrine deny any link between material security and the capacity to think and to act, but it even considers the economic insecurity of employees and their exposure to risk to be the source of their productivity and creativity. Not only does it refuse to subordinate the economy to objectives of social justice, but it makes the financial rulebook into some sort of categorical imperative for all countries, to be enforced by institutions which are themselves not democratically accountable. And not only is neo-liberal doctrine essentially hostile to the idea of social justice, but it holds that the distribution of work and its rewards is a matter for the spontaneous order of the market, and should likewise be protected from political intervention.

---

8   On the history of how a successful imitation of the real Nobel prizes, the 'Prize of the bank of Sweden in economic sciences in memory of Alfred Nobel', was established in 1969, see P. Moynot, 'Nobel d'économie: coup de maître', Le Monde, 15 Oct. 2008.

This dogmatic corpus was the predominant influence on US and British policy from the 1980s onwards, and on the European Commission from the mid-1990s. Mrs Thatcher, who introduced her policies with the rider 'TINA' (There Is No Alternative), is said to have brandished Hayek's *The Constitution of Liberty* before the House of Commons with the words, '*This* is what we believe.'[9] And when asked, after her retirement from politics, what she considered to be her greatest political achievement, she is said to have replied: 'Tony Blair'. This jibe suggests the extent to which neo-liberal ideas won over large sections of the European left. In France, a significant percentage of the economic and financial reforms inspired by the Anglo-American model were adopted by socialist governments.[10]

But neo-liberal doctrine did not merely revolutionise national legal systems. It was accompanied by neo-conservatism, which sought to construct a new international order based on principles diametrically opposed to those elaborated at the end of the Second World War. The spirit of Philadelphia advocated *cooperation* between states, in order to 'promote social progress and better standards of life in larger freedom' (UN Ch) and to ensure 'the promotion of the health, education and well-being of all peoples' (DePh). The neo-conservatives, on the other hand, chose a policy of *confrontation* with countries which did not share their world-view and of *competition* on an international scale, not only between workers but also between legal systems and cultures. The idea was to encourage each

---

9 See S. George, *Hijacking America: How the Religious and Secular Right Changed What Americans Think*, Cambridge: Polity Press, 2008, 19.
10 The Bérégovoy government (1992–1993) in France was largely responsible for deregulating the financial markets, and the Jospin government (1997–2002), with its Minister of Finance Dominique Strauss-Kahn, for introducing an Anglo-American model of corporate governance (tax benefits on stock options, companies authorised to buy back their own shares, etc.).

country to get the best out of its supposed 'comparative advantages' – a Ricardian idea – which entailed the elimination of any 'statutory obstacles' to the free play of the markets.

The central dogmas of this economic fundamentalism, as codified by international economic and financial institutions, have rapidly become a sort of official religion: the infallibility of the market, the beneficial effects of universal competition, privatisation of public services, deregulation of labour markets, and the free circulation of goods and capital. And the countless preachers of this faith can depend on today's media conglomerates to spread the word much more effectively, and tirelessly, than the pulpits of yesteryear. Both left and right governments profess the creed, despite the growing number of unbelievers and heretics.

THE METAMORPHOSES OF 'SOCIAL EUROPE'

However, it was not until the fall of communism that neo-liberal ideology, despite its political successes in the United States and Great Britain, and its adoption by international financial institutions, began to have a significant impact on the systems of solidarity established after the war in Western Europe, including public services, social protection and even wage regulation. Until that time, the distinctive feature of the European Community, in contrast to other regional customs unions, had precisely been that it aspired to more than the free circulation of goods and capital, namely the creation of a 'Social Europe' in which the free circulation of persons would go hand in hand with 'improved working conditions and an improved standard of living for workers, so as to make possible their harmonisation while the improvement is being maintained' (Treaty of Rome [1957], art. 117). The construction of a 'Social Europe' remained a goal shared by all members – with the exception of the United Kingdom, its tireless detractor – until the enlargement of the EU to former communist countries. A body of European social legislation was devised, establishing a minimum of employment protection, which individual countries were free to add to and improve. By virtue of this legislation, competition between countries and companies was reined in by a few principles of social justice, which were only waived on some points in the case of the United Kingdom. Despite the impotence and imperfections of this 'European social model', the European Community remained true to the spirit of Philadelphia until the very end of the twentieth century, whereas the communist countries had rejected it from the start, as America and the United Kingdom do today.

When former communist countries joined the EU, it was a historic opportunity to secure once and for all the principle of solidarity between peoples, and hence to breathe new life into the social model. Europe could have become a real-life testing ground of solidarity between 'rich' and 'poor' countries, that is, an international model of 'harmonisation while [the] improvement is being maintained' of working and living conditions (Treaty on European Union, art. 136 [151]). But for Europe to seize this opportunity, it would have had to conceive accession not simply as an *enlargement* but as a *reunification*.

A genuine *reunification* would have forced Europe to recognise the specific historical experience of these countries and to reflect again on how to realise the principle of social justice within a community of states having neither a common history, nor a common political culture, nor the same level of material wealth. It would have involved negotiating a new Treaty Establishing the European Community, with the West agreeing to be the principal funder of a 'Marshall Plan' for the East, and the East agreeing in return not to compete with the countries whose aid it was receiving by resorting to social and fiscal dumping.

However, since the West interpreted the collapse of the Soviet Empire as the conclusive victory of its model of society and historical proof of its unchallenged superiority, Europe chose *enlargement*, in the sense of exporting wholesale to former Eastern-bloc countries the rules prevailing in the West. In so doing, it repeated, on a much larger scale, the mistake made by the Federal Republic of Germany when it annexed the Eastern *Länder* instead of working with them to elaborate a new, foundational German constitution. Western Europe thought it could simply transplant Community legislation (the *acquis communautaire*) into countries whose histories, levels of wealth, and political and legal cultures were in every respect different from its own. And so the 'market economy' and 'social dialogue' were foisted upon countries without entrepreneurs or trade unions, and Brussels fancied it could extend its dominion over countries whose nationalistic sentiments were already inflamed by decades of subjection to Soviet imperial rule. Reunification would have forced Europe to negotiate a new social contract which took into account the real inequalities between member states, while working towards at once 'harmonisation' and 'improvement' in the living and working conditions of all European citizens. Enlargement has had quite the opposite effect: it has undermined a 'Social Europe' which already rested on fragile political foundations.

THE COMMUNIST MARKET ECONOMY

The ruling elites of the newly admitted member states, belatedly born-again free-marketeers reared on real communism, were unlikely to be receptive to the spirit of Philadelphia, its respect for the rule of law and its ideal of participatory democracy. The neo-liberal credo, on the other hand, immediately struck a chord. There they could feel on familiar ground, with the conviction that they formed an enlightened avant-garde whose mission was to force the immanent laws of the economy upon the ignorant masses and additionally bring the legal system into line with these laws. It was simply a matter of substituting the dictatorship of the markets for that of the proletariat, while leaving the conception of legality intact. Socialist legality, in the words of Soviet legal theorists, was 'the method for bringing about the dictatorship of the proletariat and the construction of socialism . . . it is always the Socialist State's means of action and cannot become an obstacle to the realisation of its historical missions'.[11] The Soviet system, years before the European Community, defined itself in terms of a process of 'construction', rather than in terms of a particular political or constitutional 'regime'.[12] This meant that it could at all times ignore its own laws in the name of a higher legality, that of 'standards of socialist conduct',[13] which only the leadership was privy to, whose content it could change at will, and whose non-observance it could sanction. One need only replace this mantra with the 'rules of a market economy in a globalised world' to understand the ease with which communists could adopt neo-liberal convictions, and to imagine the sort of normative effects such a symbiotic marriage would have.

---

11   S.A. Golunsky and M.S. Strogovitch, *Theory of State and Law*, Moscow, 1940; cit. P. Lavigne, 'La légalité socialiste et le développement de la préoccupation juridique en Union soviétique', *Revue d'Etudes Comparatives Est-Ouest* 11: 3, 1980, 11.

12   T. Kondratieva, *Gouverner et nourrir. Du pouvoir en Russie*, Paris: Les Belles Lettres, 2002.

13   In the words of the Constitution of the USSR (art. 59/130, 1936/1977): 'Citizens of the USSR are obliged to *observe the Constitution of the USSR and Soviet laws*, comply with the standards of socialist conduct, and uphold the honour and dignity of Soviet citizenship.'

The communist converts to the free market did not simply rally to the neo-liberal revolution; they also left their own distinctive stamp on it. Economic liberalism had never denied the need for a shared normative framework in the sense of the 1948 Universal Declaration's *régime de Droit*, that is, a third entity which transcends particular interests and guarantees individual rights, and whose modern incarnation is the state. In Marxist dogma, by contrast, this metaphysical being had always been branded as nothing but an instrument of the ruling class, to be attacked in capitalist lands and to serve the dictatorship of the proletariat in communist ones. This conception of the state could accommodate the dictatorship of the markets much more readily than the conception of the state as a transcendent third party, which is why it presided over the historical process by which communism and capitalism – two endeavours to Westernise the world – merged into one. But the process did not spell the disappearance of the state so much as its privatisation, its transformation into what James K. Galbraith has called a 'Corporate Republic'.[14] The metamorphosis of French political life after the 2007 presidential election is symptomatic of this transformation: forty years of governments dominated by *énarques* – products of the ENA, the fiercely competitive higher civil service graduate school – who, for all their faults, were trained in public service, gave way for the first time to a government dominated by business lawyers, trained to defend financial interests. The way in which untold sums of taxpayers' money were pumped into bankrupt financial institutions following the meltdown of the financial markets should not be interpreted as a step towards reinstating the figure of the third, the guarantor of the general interest, but rather as yet another stage in the privatisation of the state.

---

14 See J. K. Galbraith, *The Predator State*, New York: Free Press, 2008.

So European enlargement failed to win over the post-communist countries to the 'social market economy' championed by the eleven signatories to the Maastricht Treaty's social chapter, but instead enabled them to join forces with the neo-liberal camp (which had always been hostile to it). These countries' leaders could feel at home in the 'realism' of neo-liberal ideology, which, like scientific socialism, believes in the universal validity of the 'laws of the economy' and shows a similar determination to remove these laws from the political arena. The European Union thus became a perfect model of the type of 'limited democracy' so dear to Hayek. Dissenting voices, as expressed in national referendums, were silenced, in the absence of a real electoral system at Community level: the rejection of the Maastricht Treaty by Danish voters, of the Treaty of Nice by Irish voters, and of the Constitutional Treaty by French, Dutch and Irish voters was simply passed over. To consider the results of an election as binding only if they correspond to the wishes of the leaders who organised it seems to be becoming something of a habit. These sorts of practices can only increase voter apathy and discredit the sermons on democracy which Europe is so fond of delivering to the rest of the world, especially when, at the same time, the results of free elections are disqualified if they are not what the 'international community' hoped for.

Far from extending the political base of the European social model, enlargement therefore led to an attack on the spirit of Philadelphia. This occurred not only in social, but also in military and diplomatic policy, with the 'new Europe' embarking on a 'war on terror' alongside the United States and the United Kingdom, in violation of international law and human rights, and despite opposition from its own populations.

Europe is thus contributing in its own particular way to the construction, on a global scale, of what the Constitution of the People's Republic of China calls the 'communist market economy'.[15] This is a hybrid system based on what communism and capitalism had in common: abstract universalism and an economistic vision. From neo-liberal dogma it borrows the competition of all against all, the free circulation of goods and capital, and the maximisation of individual utilities, while communism contributes 'limited democracy', the instrumentalisation of the legal system (that is, the replacement of the *rule of law* with *rule by law*), an obsession with quantification and the abyss separating the lot of the rulers from that of the ruled. The ruling classes of all countries can now get astronomically rich (which was impossible under communist rule) without a thought for the fate of the middle and working classes (which was impossible under the political or social democracy of welfare states). And although the new oligarchy owes much of its sudden wealth to the privatisation of public assets, it uses market liberalisation as a pretext to exempt itself from public expenditure on national welfare systems.

This 'defection of the elites' (as Christopher Lasch aptly puts it)[16] is spearheaded by a new type of ruling class. It has little in common with the class of the traditional capitalist entrepreneur and consists of senior civil servants, former Communists and Maoist militants, who have all gone into business. Many of these leaders, in West and East alike, were raised on Marxist-Leninism or Maoism but have enthusiastically embraced the ideas of economic deregulation and the privatisation of

---

15 The exact phrase (which can be found in art. 15 of the Constitution of the People's Republic of China) is 社会主义市场经济 (*shehuizhuyi shichang jingji*), which translates literally as 'socialist market economy'. In order to avoid confusion with the meaning which 'socialist economy' has come to acquire in France (the idea of a mixed economy, which the Socialist Party espoused for a time), the translation 'communist market economy' seemed preferable.

16 C. Lasch, *The Revolt of the Elites and the Betrayal of Democracy*, New York: Norton, 1995.

public assets, which they were the first to put into practice and to profit from. This ideological pattern is clear in China, Russia and the former communist countries of Eastern Europe and Central Asia. But it also exists in Western countries, for instance at the head of the European Commission,[17] and also in France, where most of the neo-conservative evangelists are former far-left activists, and where an oligarchy could take root through the privatisation of public companies and the sky-rocketing pay packages awarded their new directors.

---

17   The president of the European Commission, José Manuel Barroso, started out as a member of the Movement to Reorganise the Party of the Proletariat, a radical Maoist group, before becoming one of the architects of the alliance between American neo-conservatives and European former communist country leaders.

2

THE PRIVATISATION OF THE WELFARE STATE

The idea of social justice is as old as the philosophy of law. Already in the fourth century BC, Aristotle deemed 'proportionate requital', a third form of justice, to be necessary for the life of the *polis*, alongside distributive and corrective justice: 'reciprocity in accordance with a proportion and not on the basis of precisely equal return. For it is by proportionate requital that the city holds together.'[1] In the early seventeenth century, Francis Bacon advanced a similar idea in his reflections on the causes of 'seditions and troubles': 'Good policy is to be used that the treasure and moneys in a state be not gathered into few hands . . . And money is like muck, not good except it be spread.'[2] In the aftermath of the Second World War, the Declaration of Philadelphia was saying much the same thing in insisting that 'lasting peace can be established only if it is based on social justice' and 'poverty anywhere constitutes a danger to prosperity everywhere'. What was new was its definition of social justice as a universal ambition and a

---

1 Aristotle, *Nicomachean Ethics*, trans. W.D. Ross, Oxford: Clarendon Press, 1908, bk V, chap. 8.
2 F. Bacon, *Essays, Civil and Moral*, New York: P.F. Collier & Son, 1909–1914; The Harvard Classics, vol. III, pt 1, chap. XV.

'fundamental objective' which should determine every nation's economic policy.

So, a course had been charted which could avoid both the devastating effects of exclusive market dominance and the liberticidal effects of exclusive state control. The Declaration of Philadelphia extended the principles of the New Deal and, far from calling for capitalism's destruction, it sought to ensure long-term market stability across the generations by providing a normative framework for the markets. In contrast to contract law, which views human beings as monads without bodies or history, social law reinstated a cross-generational dynamic, in which human beings figure on the scene of exchange complete with their physical vulnerabilities and the various affiliations which unite or divide them.

For the architects of neo-liberalism, however, the principle of social justice was a mere 'mirage',[3] and it disappeared from the agenda of globalisation when the communist regimes underwent their conversion to the market economy. But no counterrevolution can wipe out its history, and this one was no exception. When the neo-liberal counterrevolution swept over welfare states (in the West) and real communism (in the East), bent on their destruction, it brought about not the disappearance but the privatisation of the institutions of the welfare state.

The creation of a financial, technological and economic space in which national frontiers do not exist is part of the utopia of a flat world[4] in which individuals are all bearers of the same rights and are subject only to the obligations to which they freely consent. Unlike twentieth-century totalitarian utopias, this one does

3   F.A. Hayek, *Law, Legislation and Liberty: A New Statement of the Liberal Principles of Justice and Political Economy*, vol. 2: *The Mirage of Social Justice*, Chicago: University of Chicago Press, 1976.
4   T. Friedman, *The World Is Flat*, London: Penguin, 2005.

not seek to abolish individual rights. On the contrary, it supposes these to be self-sufficient, with no need to be referred to a transcendent principle of justice, since they can be defined simply by the play of differences and oppositions. As a result, any rule which comes from the outside is experienced as an imposition which should occur as infrequently as possible, and ideally not at all.

The neo-liberal agenda is therefore not the withering away of law but its deconstruction, in the postmodern sense of the term. Jacques Derrida, the father of this concept, himself maintained that the idea of justice was at heart nothing but the expression of an individual desire 'in its demand of gift without exchange . . . without calculation and without rules, without reason'; and, he continues, 'deconstruction is mad about and from such justice, mad about and from this desire for justice. Such justice, which is not law, is the very movement of deconstruction at work in law and in the history of law, in political history and history itself.'[5] This definition of justice (mad indeed), which anchors justice in individual subjectivity alone and seeks to deconstruct the law, is the philosophical counterpart of the neo-liberals' disqualification of social justice, which they accuse of being simply a sentimental aspiration and thus incapable of grounding a body of legal rules worthy of the name. Here we have an example of the profound complicity between postmodern philosophy and neo-liberalism, which converge on a fetishism of the signifier – linguistic in the first case, monetary in the second.[6]

5 J. Derrida, *Acts of Religion*, ed. Gil Anidjar, London: Routledge, 2002, 254.
6 On this critique of postmodernism, see A. Berque, *Ecoumène. Introduction à l'étude des milieux humains*, Paris: Belin, 2000, 26ff. Also, from a Marxist perspective, see N. Foé, *Le Post-modernisme et le nouvel esprit du capitalisme. Sur une philosophie globale d'empire*, Dakar: Codesria, 2008.

The legal system's 'pulverisation into individual rights'[7] opens onto a world in which individuals, for whom everything is calculable and subject to contract, jostle for position, parading identical rights. Human beings, reduced to the status of monads, should be governed by only two types of rule: rules grounded in science and rules freely self-imposed. Individual rights are doled out like weapons, in the hope that this will create an entirely contractual society, in which only self-imposed obligations exist. Whereas systematically challenging the validity of the consent of the weak to the will of the strong was the cornerstone of social legislation, its deconstruction brings back consent as the necessary and sufficient condition of legal obligation.

Another casualty of this development is the solidarity generated by social legislation. Statutory housing legislation is dismantled, while 'basic, inalienable individual rights to housing' are championed.[8] The executives of large companies receive astronomical golden handshakes, while casual workers do not even receive redundancy pay. Obligatory contributions are suddenly a worldwide imperative when it is a question of intellectual property rights, but they come under heavy fire when it is a question of financing social security schemes or public services.[9] Similarly, every reform erodes a little further the principle of a weekly day of rest, and with it the normative framework which protects a normal social and family life, while at the same time 'parental responsibility contracts' appear, to mitigate the effects on children of parents who have no time to

---

7   J. Carbonnier, *Droit et passion du droit sous la Ve République*, Paris: Flammarion, 1996, 121ff.

8   See the Council of State (*Conseil d'État*) report, *Rapport public 2009. Droit au logement, droit du logement*, Paris: LDF, 2009.

9   See the TRIPS Agreement (Trade-Related Aspects of Intellectual Property Rights) annexed to the Marrakesh Agreement establishing the World Trade Organisation.

spend with them.[10] Employment regulation is dismantled, leading to vertiginous disparities on the labour
market, yet not a year passes without the principle of
equality being invoked to justify adding yet another item
to the long list of discriminations forbidden by French
labour law. There were eighteen additions made between
1985 and 2005, an average of one every two years.
During that same period, the proportion of employees in
temporary work or on short-term contracts increased
fourfold. The destruction of qualitative differences
between persons clearly has as its corollary the legitima-
tion of quantitative differences based on the size and
stability of one's income – that is, on money.

So the privatisation of the welfare state does not
destroy social rights, but rather allows those who need
them least to benefit from them most. This is known as
the 'Matthew effect', in reference to a famous verse from
Saint Matthew's gospel ('For to everyone who has, more
will be given, and he will have abundance; but from him
who does not have, even what he has will be taken
away'). It pinpoints the capacity of the strong to take
advantage of systems designed to help the weak.[11] An
example would be the education system in France,
which on average invests much larger sums in children
from well-off families than from poorer families; or the
workers and employees who pay welfare contributions
for longer than their managers, but who can expect a
shorter retirement due to reduced life expectancy – and
the list goes on. There is nothing new about the 'Matthew
effect', but until recently it was visible only in half of the

10   See the French Code of Social Action and the Family (*Code de
l'action sociale et des familles*), art. L, 222-4-1 (Law of 31 March
2006).
11   See *Matthew* 25.29. Robert Merton was the first to highlight this
effect, with respect to research funding ('The Matthew Effect in Science',
Science 159, 1968, 56). For its relevance to welfare issues, see H. Deleeck,
'L'effet Matthieu', *Droit Social* 1979, 375; and J. Bichot, 'L'effet Matthieu
revisité', *Droit Social* 2002, 575.

equation: the rich benefited more from public spending and tax breaks than the poor. However, at the same time, the higher their income, the higher their taxes and welfare contributions. One of the novel features of the communist market economy is the emergence of an oligarchy which is able to take full advantage of social welfare systems while evading contributions proportional to their income. Neo-liberal reforms have not so much destroyed the institutions of solidarity as ushered in their pillage.

Introducing competition between national tax and welfare systems was one way of making this pillage easier, since it forced countries into a race to the bottom in their levels of compulsory contributions on higher earners. The latter can henceforth draw their income wherever obligatory deductions are lowest or non-existent, and avail themselves of the best public services and social security wherever they may be. For fifteen years now, the Court of Justice of the European Communities (CJEC), despite the fact that in theory it has no jurisdiction in matters of direct taxation, has appealed to the economic freedoms enshrined in the European Treaty to weaken member states in the face of these tax evasion strategies.[12] All countries are under pressure to lower taxation on higher earners and exempt them from contributing to the public purse in proportion to what they receive. The 'tax shield' introduced in France in 2007, despite being but one example among many, came to symbolise how proportional equality in contributing to public

12   See particularly the rulings *Bachmann* (C-204/90 of 28 Jan. 1992), *Schumacker* (C-279/93 of 14 Feb. 1995), *de Lasteyrie du Saillant* (C-9/02 of 11 March 2004), *Laboratoires Fournier* (C-39/04 of 10 March 2005) and *Manninen* (C-319/02 of 7 Sept. 2004). More recent rulings seem to have put a halt to this policy of sabotaging a country's fiscal arrangements, for example, *Krankenheim Ruhesitz am Wannsee-Seniorenheimstatt* (C-157/07 of 23 Oct. 2008, published in *Droit fiscal* 50, 2008, 616, comm. J.-Chr. Garcia).

finances was no longer being respected.[13] It protected the rich from increases in obligatory contributions, with the result that such increases were borne exclusively by the poor and the middle classes. At the same time, an increasing proportion of public money is spent protecting the assets and income of this financial oligarchy, namely through increasing the public debt. Far from reversing this trend, the meltdown of the financial markets gave it new impetus. The massive injection of public money into bankrupt banks and insurance companies, without nationalising them, is not a 'return of the state', but rather a further step in the direction of its plunder, which began already years previously in the public services, social security and employment protection.

The privatisation of the institutions of solidarity is clearest in the case of the public services. There were good reasons in the post-war years to keep away from market forces certain products and services, for example, electricity, gas, the postal service, motorways and railways, which require a single, specialised, countrywide network, which meet needs shared by all the population equally, and whose management and maintenance require a long-term vision quite different from the time-frame of the market. France had developed particularly well-adapted legal instruments in this field, mixtures of public and private law, which had proved their ability to combine economic efficiency with social justice. Given the unqualified disaster of the privatisation of public services in the Anglo-American world, one might

---

13   This measure puts a ceiling on the tax rate for the highest earners. Set at 60 percent in 2006, it was reduced to 50 percent of taxable income in 2007 by the law called 'Work Employment Purchasing Power' (*Travail Emploi Pouvoir d'Achat* [TEPA], 21 Aug. 2007). As a result, in 2008, 834 beneficiaries with assets of over €15.5 million received an average of €368,261 each from the state.

reasonably have expected these structures to be developed further rather than privatised. The obstinacy with which privatisation was nevertheless pursued in France cannot be explained simply by blind belief in neo-liberalism and pressure from the European Commission. It was above all pushed through by top managers and shareholders who looked to make substantial gains through the privatisation of companies which would thereafter have a de facto monopoly and a captive customer base.

Another aspect of this plunder of public services is the marked decline in the ethos of public service. In a centralised country like France, the integrity of its key administrative bodies is crucial to a sense of justice in society at large.[14] Their disinterested commitment to the public good is meant to radiate throughout the machinery of state and affect even the lowliest of its servants. The duties incumbent upon the holders of public office (what in the Middle Ages was called the *officium*) were what justified the advantages they were granted (called the *beneficium*). This spirit of public service lost credibility when top civil servants began to convert to market values (under the name of 'New Public Management') and moved into the private sector, such that they could keep the benefits of office without shouldering the burdens, coming to embody cynicism and greed. It is hardly surprising that those who make a clean sweep of all the benefits of high office will have difficulty getting their message across when they preach austerity to those who have fallen on

14   If we were to hazard an analogy to characterise the rise and fall of our 'elites', the Chinese celestial bureaucracy would be apter than the European *ancien régime* nobility. See J. Gernet, *L'intelligence de la Chine. Le social et le mental*, Paris: Gallimard, 1994, esp. 31ff.; and by the same author, 'Organisation, principes et pratiques de l'administration chinoise (11°–19° s.)', in *Servir l'Etat*, Paris: Éd. de l'EHESS, 1987, 11ff.; and E. Balazs, *La bureaucratie céleste*, Paris: Gallimard, 1968.

hard times. And this egoism is contagious. 'Maximising one's individual utility', clinging to one's privileges or what is left of them and taking it easy rather than driving oneself hard, has become a national sport. The inability to do without the state is matched only by the inability to continue to trust it. The civil service and the public services, which are in many respects the backbone of a country like France, are today under a twofold threat of ossification and disintegration: ossification, when the status quo is upheld by people who are more concerned to protect their acquired privileges than to serve the public interest; and disintegration, due to the – often far from disinterested – zealots of privatisation or of modelling public services on the for-profit sector.

The greatest financial gains to be made from carving up the welfare state were in the field of social security. Pension schemes were targeted with particular insistence by the financial oligarchy, which set out to turn welfare-state institutions into private profit. In the countries where these institutions were privatised, the stock-market lottery was kept buoyant, while the workers who had financed them were exposed to the risk – amply proven today – of receiving only pitiful sums in retirement. Where contributory pension schemes were maintained, casual workers suffered most from the reforms introduced, while top executives employed by multinationals received lavish 'top-up' pensions. But the pillage of solidarity schemes is a general trend evident in all branches of social security. For example, one of the reasons for the current state of bankruptcy of the health insurance system in France is the strength of the medical lobby. The profession is financed essentially by national contributions, but it refuses to accept any constraints on its activities in return. Another example is unemployment benefit, which has been siphoned off towards companies at the expense of the unemployed, in the name of 'activating' unemployment expenditure. When traders on London's stock exchange lost the jobs in which they had helped bring the financial markets to collapse, they were able, courtesy of EU welfare legislation, to claim French unemployment benefits from schemes into which they had never paid insurance contributions; the sums involved were four times the social security's limit (totalling €6,366.80 per month, as of September 2008).[15] At the other extreme, that of the working poor, the woman who goes from one insecure part-time job to another will have a hard time cobbling together a sufficiently long period of welfare contributions to be eligible for unemployment benefits, and, with the latest pension reforms, she will have lost all hope of getting a decent pension.

However, the social security system, although battered, has on the whole managed to resist this wilful deconstruction of the welfare state better than most. The mechanisms of solidarity have proved remarkably robust, at least in 'Old Europe', in the face of the violent attacks on them for their excessive cost or the constraints on individual freedoms they represent. So any serious account of the effects of three decades of neo-liberal policy on social security systems should be careful not to amalgamate the risks covered and the countries concerned. In France, for example, at the cost of often gruelling negotiations between social partners and the state, the reforms introduced have managed to protect retirement and unemployment insurance schemes. In the case of health insurance, however, the coffers are empty, principally because successive governments have proved incapable of adopting reforms that were in the general interest rather than aimed at short-term electoral gains.

Lastly, it is employment protection measures which suffer most visibly from the 'Matthew effect' today. The

---

15   *Le Point*, 19 Sept. 2008.

reforms designed to adapt these to the market did not get rid of historically acquired privileges, but rather eroded or destroyed protection where it was most necessary, while benefits continued to pile up for the higher earners. Top executives availed themselves of mechanisms developed in labour law, such as severance pay, supplementary pension payments and employee shareholding, to award themselves colossal sums even as they steered the large companies they were piloting into bankruptcy. At the other end of the scale, employment protection is the most visible example of how the state, business and finance have switched positions. Formerly, the centralised state laid down guidelines for economic policy, which the business world implemented and financial institutions supported. Nowadays, business strategy is determined by financial gains, while the costs in terms of human casualties are borne by the state, either directly, in the form of the financing of its employment policies, or indirectly, when it has to deal with poverty, violence and insecurity.

People in employment through government-supported schemes are not characterised in law as *occupying* the post they hold but as *beneficiaries* of the job. Such 'benefits' are skimpy indeed, rarely more than a minimum wage for full-time work (€1,337.70 gross, that is, roughly €1,050 net per month, as of 1 July 2009). Yet at the same time, 'value creation' has become divorced from labour and instead designates the sums – truly 'beneficial' this time – paid out by companies to their shareholders. It is indeed a topsy-turvy world where work is represented as the effect, not the cause, of wealth. But this illusion is nothing new: in around 1000 AD, Bishop Adalbero dedicated a poem to Robert the Pious, King of France, in which he deplored that 'the master, who claims to feed his serf, is fed by him. And the serf never sees an end to his tears and sighs.'[16]

---

16   Cit. Jacques Le Goff, *Medieval Civilization 1400–1500*, trans. Julia Barrow, Oxford: Blackwell, 1988, 255–6.

3

THE TOTAL MARKET

The market can only be regarded as a general regulatory principle of economic life, if the planet, labour and money are treated *as though* they were commodities, which of course is not the case.[1] The market economy thus rests on legal fictions, but ones which are not the stuff of novels. These fictions are only sustainable if they are humanly viable. If we did not have environmental legislation to protect our natural resources in the real world, we could not go on much longer treating nature as though it were a commodity. And if we did not have social legislation to protect our 'human resources', labour markets would not have long to live. When the Declaration of Philadelphia affirmed that 'labour is not a commodity' and demanded 'the extension of social security measures to provide a basic income to all in need of such protection and comprehensive medical care', it was exhorting nations to adopt labour legislation and a social security system which would guarantee the physical and economic security of employees and their families – in other words, it was

---

1 Cf. K. Polanyi, 'The Self-Regulating Market and the Fictitious Commodities: Labor, Land, and Money', in *The Great Transformation: The Political and Economic Origins of Our Time*, Boston: Beacon Press, 1944, 71–80.

establishing the legal foundations required for the labour market to remain functional in the long term, across the generations.

Such legal foundations were established at the national level and are being eroded daily by the process of globalisation. The same is true of the money markets, whose systematic deregulation was carried out with a thoroughness whose devastating effects we are only just beginning to grasp. When these legal mechanisms give way, the market economy ceases to be anchored in the real diversity of people, territories and products. One can continue for a time to behave *as though* the planet, labour and money exist independently of natural environments, workers and the real economy, but these fictions will end up being overtaken by the reality principle. Free market devotees naively believe that dismantling national legal systems will allow the 'spontaneous order of *the* market' to prevail, but in fact it will do quite the opposite and destroy the foundations of *all* markets. There is no such thing as the Free Market, but instead a range of legal instruments underpinning different types of markets, depending on the nature of the products and services exchanged, but also on the specific histories and legal cultures involved.

If we want a snapshot of how the institutional bases of markets are being sapped today, we should be careful to distinguish between two separate phenomena which have been amalgamated under the fetishised term 'globalisation'. The abolition of physical distances through the circulation of data between people is a structural phenomenon made possible by the new digital technologies. The free circulation of goods and capital, on the other hand, is a conjunctural phenomenon which is the outcome of reversible political decisions (the lifting of trade barriers) and of temporary overuse of non-renewable physical resources (keeping transport costs artificially low). It is the combination of these two different phenomena which creates the utopia of a Total Market. In this market, people, signs and things are all destined to be made commensurable, and mobilised – 'liquidated', in the legal sense – for worldwide competition.[2]

This market is *total* in Ernst Jünger's sense when, in the wake of the First World War, he referred to a mode of organisation based on the mobilisation of absolutely all human, technological and material resources, with a view to 'producing armies on the assembly line that they sent to the battlefield both day and night, where an equally mechanical bloody maw took over the role of consumer'.[3] It was during the Great War that men were first transformed into fuel to feed a monotonously functioning war-machine, like a 'turbine fueled with blood'. Thereafter, this mode of organisation – to ensure that every being or thing could be converted into units of available energy – became the norm. It was the birth of a managerial universe which is still ours today, and which Jünger described in 1932 in the following terms:

> What characterises our situation is that our movements are ruled by the constraint of maintaining our record and by the ever-widening scope of the criterion of minimal performance demanded. This fact makes it impossible for any walk of life whatsoever to settle into a predictable and reliable order. Instead, our way

---

2   A debt or a debt claim is termed 'liquid' when it can be converted into a certain quantity of money. Liquidating an asset means making it fungible, converting it into monetary rights. In everyday language, French *liquide* refers both to ready money (cash) and to anything which flows, like water, and is without form.

3   E. Jünger, 'Total Mobilization', in *The Heidegger Controversy: A Critical Reader*, ed. Richard Wolin, trans. Joel Golb and Richard Wolin, Cambridge, Mass.: MIT Press, 1993, 128–9. This seminal article later inspired Carl Schmitt and his concept of the total state.

of life resembles a deadly race in which our energies
must be stretched to the utmost if we are not to be left
behind.[4]

Legal systems integrated economic competitiveness as
their ultimate goal because they adhered to the dogma
that increased production and trade were ends in themselves, and that these ends could only be met by
introducing all-out global competition. The very first
lines of the Marrakesh Agreement which founded the
World Trade Organisation (WTO), spell this out. The
trade relations between countries should 'be conducted
with a view to raising standards of living, ensuring full
employment and a large and steadily growing volume
of real income and effective demand, and expanding
the production of and trade in goods and services'. The
contrast with the Declaration of Philadelphia is striking. For the WTO, the growth in quantifiable economic
indicators (employment levels, 'a large and steadily
growing volume' of income and demand) and 'expanding the production of and trade in goods and services'
are treated as ends in themselves. Human beings are
not so much as mentioned among the goals assigned to
the economy and to trade, nor are the associated values
of human freedom, dignity, economic security and
spiritual life.

Moreover, when we look at how these objectives may
be met, the chasm separating the two texts is even more
striking. The goals of the Marrakesh Agreement can be
achieved 'by entering into reciprocal and mutually
advantageous arrangements directed to the substantial
reduction of tariffs and other barriers to trade and to
the elimination of discriminatory treatment in international trade relations' (para. 3 of the Preamble). In
the Declaration of Philadelphia, by contrast, the rules

---

4 E. Jünger, *Der Arbeiter; Herrschaft und Gestalt*, Hamburg:
Hanseatische Verlagsanstalt, [ca. 1932].

governing trade are simply means whose effectiveness can be assessed in terms of the degree of social justice they enable countries to realise. The hierarchy between means and ends simply disappears in the Marrakesh Agreement, as do any mechanisms for measuring – in terms of the standard of living, employment rates, or income – how efficient it is to extend the free circulation of goods and capital to the whole planet. When removing trade barriers is conceived as an end in itself – as this new dogma has it – any assessment of its real effects becomes unnecessary, and when generalised competition is the goal, human beings are simply the means to attain it. And not a word of the need for international action in order to 'avoid severe economic fluctuations [and] to assure greater stability in world prices of primary products' (DePh, art. IV). Competition must know no bounds and must spur on individuals, companies and countries alike to cultivate their 'comparative advantage'.[5]

DARWINIAN LEGAL SELECTION

Legal systems – just like religions, ideas or the arts[6] – are viewed by the total market as products competing globally, in order to ensure the natural selection of those best adapted to the requirement of attractive returns. No longer is free competition grounded in a legal system, but legal systems are the offspring of free competition. This Darwinism in the normative sphere

---

5   On this managerial watchword taken from Ricardo, see M. Porter, *The Competitive Advantage of Nations*, New York: Free Press, 1990. Compare J.K. Galbraith, *The Predator State*, New York: Free Press, 2008, 69ff.

6   See R.H. Coase, 'The Market for Goods and the Market for Ideas', *The American Economic Review* 64, 1974, 384–91. On the US Supreme Court's application of this concept of the 'market of ideas' to religions, see L. Mayali (ed.), *Le façonnage juridique du marché des religions aux Etats-Unis*, Paris: Mille et une nuits, 2002.

had been theorised by Hayek when, in his mistrust of the 'rational actor' in economics, he turned to the natural selection of normative systems through competition between rights and cultures on a global scale. In his view, Social Darwinism was wrong to focus on the selection of congenitally fitter individuals, because the time scale involved was too long, and the theory neglected 'the decisively important selective evolution of rules and practices'.[7]

In the economic sphere, the freedoms associated with free trade (freedom of establishment, freedom to supply services and to put goods and capital into circulation) have been used to justify investors and companies dodging the legislation of the countries in which they operate in favour of other, more profitable, ones. Flags of convenience, which used to be confined to the law of the sea, have been raised on dry land in the form of a 'law shopping' which treats national legislation as a product competing on an international market of norms.[8] This approach was actively promoted in Europe by the CJEC, which upheld a company's right to dodge the rules of the country in which it was operating by registering in a country with less restrictive rules.[9] The legal view of the world implicit in these developments is that of a market of norms where free individuals may choose

7   F.A. Hayek, *Law, Legislation and Liberty: A New Statement of the Liberal Principles of Justice and Political Economy*, vol. 3: *The Political Order of a Free People*, Chicago: University of Chicago Press, 1979, 154.

8   A. Supiot, 'Le droit du travail bradé sur le marché des normes', *Droit social*, 2005, 1087ff. For an overview and numerous references, see H. Muir Watt, *Aspects économiques du droit international privé (Réflexions sur l'impact de la globalisation économique sur les fondements des conflits de lois et de juridictions)*, Académie de droit international de La Haye, *Recueil des cours* 307 (2004), Leiden and Boston: Martinus Nijhoff, 2005.

9   CJEC, 9 March 1999, *Centros*, Case C-212/97, European Court Reports 1999, I-1459, concl. La Pergola.

to be subject to the law which is most profitable to
them.

In order to help the law shoppers choose within
this market, the '*Doing Business*' programme of the
World Bank has been publishing a yearly report since
2004 which evaluates the economic efficiency of
national legal systems.[10] The regularly updated data-
base of figures is supposed to supply us with an
'objective measure' of legal systems in 178 countries
(renamed 'economies'). One of its quantifiable indicators is the 'rigidity' of a country's employment
legislation. In the 2005 Report, for example, one can
find a chapter entitled *Hiring and Firing Workers*,
which is devoted to the extent to which this legislation might discourage investment in a given country.
The comparative table of all the labour regulation in
the world includes the following indicators: difficulties in hiring; difficulties in extending or reducing
working time; difficulties in making a worker redun-
dant; employment rigidity; and the costs of hiring
and firing.[11] Needless to say, regulation goes by the
name of 'difficulties' or 'rigidities', and employee
rights, by the name of 'costs'. Countries which confer
too many rights on their labour force score badly in
the 'employment rigidity' index, for example those
with social protection for part-time employees, where
minimum wages are considered too high (20 dollars
a month, the World Bank opines, is excessive for an
African country), where the working week is limited
to 66 hours and where there exist such things as

10   See doingbusiness.org, where one can find a globe representing the
earth as a sphere of legislative areas in competition: 'Business planet
mapping the business environment'.
11   See doingbusiness.org/ExploreTopics/HiringFiringWorkers/Compare
All.aspx. The World Bank uses a methodology developed by Harvard
and Yale University economists. See J. Botero, S. Djankov, R. La Porta,
F. Lopez-de-Silanes and A. Shleifer, 'The Regulation of Labor', *Quarterly
Journal of Economics*, Nov. 2004.

redundancy notice or schemes for tackling racial or sexual discrimination.[12]

The introduction of this 'market in legal products' will in the long run eliminate the normative systems which are the least able to satisfy the financial expectations of investors. Competition for the favour of the financial markets will extend beyond the economic sphere and become the organisational principle of the legal order as well. In France, this Darwinistic approach is welcomed by the country's highest court,[13] and what criticism it receives centres not on the principle but on the 'score' attributed (continental legal systems are deemed 'less competitive' than common law ones).[14]

Since the accession of post-communist countries to the European Union, competition between the national welfare and fiscal regimes of member states has been introduced, as recommended by the Open Method of Coordination (ratified by the Treaty of Amsterdam).[15] This technique of governance aims to transplant the broad principles of the EU's economic policy into the realm of social protection, particularly to make

---

12 Under fire particularly from the trade union grouping Global Unions (global-unions.org), the World Bank backed down in 2009 on its 'Employing Workers Indicators', stating that it would rework them in consultation with the ILO.

13 See the official opening speech for the new session of the *Cour de cassation* in 2005. It was given by the Court's President (subsequently nominated to sit on the Constitutional Council), who welcomed the notion of a 'market of codifications' and called for 'credible indicators' to prove the 'world competitiveness' of the French judicial system. (G. Canivet, 'Vers une nouvelle pensée juridique', *Les Cahiers du débat*, March 2005.)

14 See the Association Henri Capitant, *Les droits de tradition civiliste en question. A propos des Rapports* Doing Business *de la Banque mondiale*, Société de législation comparée, 2006. Available online on the website of the Association: henricapitant.org/node/77.

15 EU Treaty, art. 125ff. See P. Pochet, 'La stratégie européenne pour l'emploi en 2001', *Droit social* 2001, 1090ff.; S. de la Rosa, 'Stratégie européenne pour l'emploi: les nouvelles orientations', *Droit social* 2005, 1210ff.

labour forces adapt to the demands of the markets. The 'performance' of EU member states with respect to the targets set is measured by a battery of quantifiable performance indicators developed by the Commission and is regularly scrutinised in peer-review sessions. This is how member states are encouraged to improve their statistical score, and the technique of benchmarking is used to urge the dunces of the European classroom to emulate the star pupils.

This 'soft' pressure to compete, which does not take the form of legislation, operates in conjunction with the pressures applied by the CJEC. This institution, although little known to the media or the general public, has significant legislative power in the European Union. It resembles the sovereign courts of the *ancien régime* or the high court under a common law system, in that it decides for the future through general provisions applicable to all, just like legislation. Whereas in the European Parliament or on the European Council, countries have representation in proportion to their population, the CJEC is composed of one judge per member state. This is why, given the ideological alliance forged between the post-communist and neo-liberal countries that comprise the 'New Europe', the Court has proved a particularly powerful instrument for implementing the communist market economy. The European Treaty's aim of 'harmonisation while [the] improvement is being maintained', which informed the Court's previous case-law, has been abandoned in favour of allowing companies established in member states with low wages and weak social protection to exploit their 'comparative advantages' to the full. It has done this by allowing companies to ignore collective agreements[16] and the laws which index salaries

---

16   CJEC, 18 Dec. 2007, Case C-341/05, *Laval*; 3 April 2008, Case C-346/06, *Rüffert*, which allows foreign workers who have been seconded to jobs in an EU country to be paid half the rate stipulated in the country's collective agreements.

to the cost of living;[17] it has dismissed the presumption
of salaried status enshrined in the laws of the foreign
countries in which these companies operate;[18] it has
condemned legal measures which ensure that the rights
of workers in host countries can be adequately
monitored;[19] it has claimed that flags of convenience are
a question of freedom of establishment;[20] and in principle it has outlawed strike action against relocations.[21] In
one of its recent judgements along these lines, the CJEC
decided that the goal of protecting social harmony and
the purchasing power of workers did not constitute public
imperatives sufficiently important to justify infringing
the principle of an unrestricted 'freedom to provide' services.[22] What more eloquent expression of how far we
have moved away from the spirit of Philadelphia!

THE RACE TO THE BOTTOM IN SOCIAL PROTECTION

Competition between bodies of norms is most visible, on
a global scale, in the phenomenon of relocation.
Relocation also shows how, paradoxically, this competition actually perverts the principle of free competition. If
a company decides to set up abroad in order to win a
share of the market, it will be competing with other companies, and all will be subject to the rules governing the
market in question. If the business is successful, its investment will bring returns and will also benefit populations
locally. Freedom to invest and free competition in this
instance contribute to improving people's material
well-being. When, on the other hand, a business relocates

---

17   CJEC, 19 June 2008, Case C-319/06, *Commission v. Grand Duchy
of Luxembourg.*
18   CJEC, 15 June 2006, Case C-255/04, *Commission v. France.*
19   CJEC, 19 June 2008, Case C-319/06, *Grand Duchy of Luxembourg.*
20   CJEC, 6 Dec. 2007, Case C-438/05, *Viking.*
21   CJEC, 6 Dec. 2007, Case C-438/05, *Viking.*
22   CJEC, 19 June 2008, Case C-319/06, *Commission v. Grand Duchy
of Luxembourg.*

its activities and then re-imports the products it has made in breach of the fiscal, employment and environmental rules of its home country, one can no longer talk of competition between products (short of believing that the company competes with itself), but of competition between normative systems. With the result, which no one can any longer ignore, that countries struggle to undercut one another precisely in their fiscal, employment and environmental legislation, and those initially 'benefiting' from relocations are rapidly abandoned as soon as less stringent legislation appears elsewhere.[23]

Once the CJEC had abandoned the goal for Europe of improving 'living and working conditions, so as to make possible their harmonization while the improvement is being maintained' (Treaty on the Functioning of the EU, art. 151), it got down to eliminating any obstacles to the dismantling of social protection, as the *Viking* and *Laval* judgements of late 2007 testify.[24] On the one hand the Court declared that the right to strike 'constitutes a fundamental right which forms an integral part of the general principles of Community law', but on the other it refused to apply this principle in order to oblige the businesses from country A operating in country B to respect all its laws and collective agreements. Barring an 'imperative reason in the public interest', trade unions must do nothing which could render 'less attractive, or even pointless' the practice of relocations and flags of convenience.

This jurisprudence throws into harsh relief the course democracy has taken in the European Union. We already knew that the European citizen had almost no purchase on Community legislation, both due to the fact that no real electoral system exists at the Community level and because of member states'

23   See J.-L. Gréau, *L'avenir du capitalisme*, Paris: Gallimard, 2005, 212ff.
24   CJEC, 6 Dec. 2007, Case C-438/05, *Viking*; and CJEC, 18 Dec. 2007, Case C-341/05, *Laval*.

proclivity for ignoring the results of national referenda on Community treaties. To which should now be added the *Laval* and *Viking* rulings, which outlaw strikes and other forms of trade union action if they disrupt the 'spontaneous order' of the market. The Court ruled that 'the abolition, as between Member States, of obstacles to freedom of movement for persons and freedom to provide services would be compromised if the abolition of State barriers could be neutralised by obstacles resulting from the exercise, by associations or organisations not governed by public law [i.e. trade unions], of their legal autonomy'.[25] In so doing, it was effectively stating that trade union activity should henceforth be governed by commercial law, in violation of the principle that workers and employers may 'exercise freely the right to organise', as laid down in Convention 87 of the ILO.

Freedom of association is, however, no minor component of a democracy. Whereas the social policies of corporatist or communist countries were on occasion more generous or ambitious than those of Western democracies, the hallmark of these despotic regimes was that their vision of a common good was imposed from above and could not be contested. Trade unions were obliged to accept economic dogmas to the effect that the status quo was by definition just. What characterises a democracy, by contrast, is the idea that social justice cannot simply be imposed from above, but must also proceed from below, from the conflicting interests of employers and employees. This leads to a real and not only a formal recognition and protection of the freedom to associate and the right to strike, so that the weak may challenge the 'justice' of the strong. Significantly, the right to strike was enshrined in law in Western democracies only after the Second World War, which is an indication of how fragile it is in

---

25   CJEC, 18 Dec. 2007, Case C-341/05, *Laval*, § 98.

Western Europe. And since this right has no purchase at all in post-communist countries, it is hardly surprising that, after European enlargement, the European Court, contrary to what it had decided a few years previously concerning collective agreements,[26] ruled that the collective freedoms of employees would henceforth be subordinate to the economic freedoms of business enterprises.

Such rulings may push Europe still further down a dangerous path. The legal instruments characteristic of democracies, whether electoral freedom or freedom to associate, allow potential political and social violence to be metabolised, and power relations to be converted into forms of law. By blocking these processes, and by making competition into the one and only principle that makes the whole world go round, we are heading for the same impasses as those we have already witnessed in twentieth-century totalitarianisms, all of which enslaved their legal orders to the supposed laws of the economy, history or biology. This claim, and the prediction that such a doctrine will inevitably generate irrationality and violence, are not dictated by some political or moral stance. Rather, they stem from one of the rare certainties that the 'science of law' can contribute: precisely because egoism, greed and the struggle for life are well and truly present in this world *as it is*, they must be contained and channelled by a common reference to the world *as it should be*. This distinction between is and ought, *Sein* and *Sollen*,[27] has been the target of scientism in all its forms for more than a century, as it attempts to assimilate legal rules to technical norms. But these attempts have always ended up as failures and bloodbaths. Historical fact may of course

---

26 CJEC, 21 Sept. 1999, Case C-67/96, *Albany*, § 60.
27 See on this point the insightful article by L. Kolakowski, 'The Persistence of the Sein-Sollen Dilemma', *Man and World: Continental Philosophy Review* 10, 1977, 194–233.

show that competition between classes, races and individuals does exist, but to make universal struggle into the founding principle of legal systems is to negate the legal order as such and to set humanity on the road to ruin. It also leads to loss of contact with reality, since dogma, which previously resided on high in the realm of values, now permeates the pseudo-scientific representation of the world underpinning our faith in 'governance'.

4

THE MIRAGE OF
QUANTIFICATION

In economic theory, 'the market' is regarded as a model of self-regulation, similar to what science (the true science) observes in living beings and what technology (particularly computing) introduces into machines. For Marxist sociology no less than neo-liberal economics, the market expresses the immanent laws of human behaviour, which can be generalised beyond the marketplace. Everything seems to lend itself to analysis in terms of supply, demand, competition, capital, products and price, from the 'marriage market' to the 'market of ideas'.[1] This extension of market logic to the life of society in its entirety encourages human beings to be viewed as '"particles" . . . that are under the sway of forces of attraction, of repulsion, and so on, as in a magnetic field'.[2] The upheavals in belief systems in the wake of the Second World War did not manage to uproot the conviction that human beings can be explained scientifically, which in turn could make their behaviour strictly programmable and make

---

1 See, for example, G.S. Becker, 'Altruism, Egoism, and Genetic Fitness: Economics and Sociobiology', art. cit.; and P. Bourdieu, *Distinction: A Social Critique of the Judgment of Taste*, Cambridge, Mass.: Harvard University Press, 1984.

2 P. Bourdieu and L. Wacquant, *An Invitation for Reflexive Sociology*, Chicago: University of Chicago Press, 1992, 106.

legal dogma a thing of the past. Pre-war scientisms, which sought in the laws of history or race the way to rule people, simply gave way to belief in a world where the calculation of utility would reign supreme. It was yet another version of the old dream of being able to govern human beings as though they were things.

This dream results from a confusion, pinpointed by the great historian of science Georges Canguilhem, between the regulation of machines or biological organisms and that of human societies.[3] Boilers or amoebas obey internal regulatory principles, but an ordered human society will always refer to norms external to any of its members. Such external norms, be they legal or religious, can be postulated, displayed and celebrated, but they cannot be scientifically demonstrated.

Today's version of scientism ignores this fundamental distinction. It sees a world in which no laws exist except those of physics, and in which man holds no secrets for himself. An example of this thinking can be found in the glossy Annual Report of the French National Centre for Scientific Research (CNRS), which devotes a few pages to 'knowledge of the human being'. Recently, this section has borne the title, in huge type, 'HOW DOES THE HUMAN BEING WORK?' In the Centre's 2006 report, the answer is contained in the subtitle: *'The human being works on the electricity which goes through its neurons, and the communication this produces. Researchers are attempting the incredible feat of getting the brain to understand its own workings – and, increasingly, they are being successful.'*[4] In this

3   G. Canguilhem, 'Le problème des régulations dans l'organisme et dans la société', *Cahiers de l'Alliance israëlite universelle* 92, Sept.–Oct. 1955, 64ff.; repr. in *Écrits sur la médecine*, Paris: Seuil, 2002, 108ff.
4   *2006. Une année avec le CNRS*, Paris: CNRS, 2006, 18–19 (emphasis in the original). It is unlikely that the authors of this text have read Saint Augustine, but in any case it is clear that they are immune to the doubt which beset him, and which psychoanalysis – a discipline

grandiose vision, there is nothing in the world which cannot be calculated and programmed. The world 'runs on communication', not conversation. It is flat and without mystery. And it is a world in which the universe of signs would correspond perfectly to the universe of things, such that the question of the sense of human life would at last be senseless.[5]

GOVERNANCE BY NUMBERS

In such a world, government by laws gives way to governance by numbers. Government by laws aims at the application of general and abstract rules which secure a person's identity, freedoms and duties. It relies on the faculty of *judgement* – that is, on acts of legal *qualification* (distinguishing different situations and submitting them to different rules) and on the *interpretation* of texts (whose meaning can never be fixed once and for all). Governance by numbers, on the other hand, aims at producing a self-regulating human society. It relies on *calculation* – that is, on acts of *quantification* (subsuming different beings and situations under the same unit of account) and on *programming* behaviour (through techniques of benchmarking and ranking). Governance obliterates the vertical dimension of normativity; the law is no longer that which transcends fact, but that which may be inferred from measuring fact.

This goal of reducing the diversity of beings and things to measurable quantities is integral to the project

---

banished from the CNRS – has corroborated, namely in the question: 'Is the mind, then, too narrow to grasp itself?' (*Confessions* X, 8.15; see Saint Augustine, trans. Maria Boulding, New York: New City Press, 1997, 246–7.)

5 This utopia was prefigured in E. Abbott's novel, *Flatland: A Romance of Many Dimensions*, first published in 1884. O. De Leonardis shows how strikingly relevant it is today, in 'Nuovi conflitti a Flatlandia', in G. Grossi (ed.), *Conflitti contemporanei*, Turin: Utet, 2008, 5ff.

of a total market, which seeks to encompass all of humankind and all the products of the planet, and in which all countries would abolish their trade barriers and exploit their 'comparative advantages'. 'The elimination of discriminatory treatment in international trade relations', which the WTO has set its heart on, requires the heterogeneity of national legal systems to be reduced and any rules liable to hinder the free circulation of goods and capital to be abolished. The environmental effects of removing barriers to trade are already visible. These are by no means exhausted by the high-profile cases in which countries were condemned for banning imports of goods produced using methods which infringed their own environmental legislation.[6] The levelling of differences extends to the whole planet, which is assimilated to a commodity and so must be made available for investment and real estate speculation. In the words of the CJEC, 'The purchase of immovable property in a Member State by a non-resident ... constitutes an investment in real estate which falls within the category of capital movements between Member States. Freedom for such movements is guaranteed by [the] Treaty.'[7] This transformation of the earth into an asset which can be liquidated on a global market explains why the notion of space, which was previously confined in legal terminology to parts of the world which had no definable limits and were unfit for human habitation, and so could not be occupied on a long-term basis (seas and oceans, the air and interstellar space), has recently been introduced into land law. The European Union, in

6 See the famous cases of tuna or shrimp fished with nets which destroy dolphins and sea turtles. On this ruling, see R. Howse and D. Regan, 'The Product/Process Distinction – An Illusory Basis for Disciplining "Unilateralism"', in *Trade Policy: European Journal of International Law* 11: 2, 2000, 249–89.
7 CJEC, 13 July 2000, *Alfredo Albore*, Case C-423/98; *European Court Reports*, 2000, I-05965.

establishing a single market, was the first to give itself a legal definition as an '*area* of freedom, security and justice'. It was no longer to be a single territory or group of discrete territories, with clearly identifiable borders, but would henceforth be open to an indeterminate and indeterminable number of new member states.[8]

Of course, globalisation cannot ignore the *actual* diversity of landscapes, human environments, ways of life, languages, cultural treasures and modes of thought. Since, unlike commodities – and what the market economy assimilates to commodities, like work, land and money – their value cannot be fixed by the market, their preservation and renewal should in principle be governed by the *lex loci*. Yet the global market still considers them as resources to be taken into account when determining the comparative advantage of a country or a region of the globe. This is why new techniques designed to quantify and measure the relative value of these non-market goods and find a universal unit of measurement for them have materialised. Such techniques of scoring are applied today in fields as diverse as scientific research (bibliometrics), comparative law (for the purposes of 'law shopping', see chapter 3) and 'human development'. Geographical elements such as towns, nations and territories are treated as though they were competing trademarks, giving rise to the notion of 'nation branding', established on the basis of quantitative indicators of 'local identity capital'.[9] This means that local identity has to be

8 Whereas the notion of space did not figure in the Treaty of Rome signed in 1957, it was introduced into the 1986 Single European Act (see art. 2, art. 14 and art. 154 of the Consolidated Treaty). See also A. Supiot, 'The Territorial Inscription of Laws', in *Soziologische Jurisprudenz, Festschrifte für Gunther Teubner*, Berlin: De Gruyter, 2009, 375–93.

9 See L. Doria, 'La qualità totale del territorio: verso una fenomenologia critica', *Archivio di studi urbani e regionali* 80, 11–56; L. Doria, V. Fedeli and C. Tedesco, *Rethinking European Spatial Policy*

broken down into a normalised set of features which
may be evaluated (landscape, climate, public infra-
structures, public safety, cuisine, etc.), and that local
political and economic 'players' then vie with one
another to improve their 'territorial competitiveness'
score.

THE PITFALLS OF SELF-REFERENCE

In our attempts to transform every singular quality
into a measurable quantity, we become enclosed in a
speculative circle, where belief in quantitative representations gradually supplants any contact with the
realities to which these representations are supposed to
refer. We can only count identifiable objects to which
we give a similar qualification, and the categories of
thought through which we identify and classify natural
objects are not themselves mathematical (which does
not mean that this identification and classification are
irrational). The labour of thought involves endowing
calculation with sense by systematically relating the
quantities measured to a sense of measure. The need to
relate any calculation to a system of references placed
beyond calculation is even more essential when one
tries to measure economic and social fact, rather than
simply natural phenomena. Alain Desrosières's groundbreaking work has shown that economic and social
statistics do not measure a pre-existing reality, unlike
statistics in the natural sciences, but construct a new
reality by positing equivalence between heterogeneous
beings and forces.[10] Statistical information resembles a
legal constitution in that it is essentially normative and

---

as a Hologram, Aldershot: Ashgate Publisher, 2006, 235ff.
10   A. Desrosières, The Politics of Large Numbers: A History of
Statistical Reasoning, trans. Camille Naish, Cambridge, Mass.: Harvard
University Press, 1998; and by the same author, Pour une sociologie
historique de la quantification, Paris: Presses de l'École des Mines, 2007.

serves to construct a public realm. However, unlike a constitution, its normativity is hidden from view. Statistics are unable to integrate the dimension of change, and 'the "incontrovertible facts" which they are called upon to supply (but which in fact they help to ratify) do not contain the modalities of how they may be debated'.[11]

When we conflate measuring and evaluating, we are bound to lose a sense of measure. Evaluation is not simply measurement, since it refers measurement to a value judgement which gives it meaning. There is necessarily a dogmatic dimension to how this meaning is defined, since our categories of thought are not a gift of nature, but rather a means of comprehending it. Modern auditing procedures seem to have completely forgotten the wise warning given by one of the fathers of modern accounting, James Anyon, at the end of the nineteenth century: 'Use figures as little as you can . . . Think and act upon facts, truths and principles and regard figures only as things to express these . . . The well trained and experienced accountant of today is not a man of figures.'[12] If the market, as the realm of the calculable, is to function properly, it must be referred to a norm which lies outside calculation. Failing this, as the recent collapse of the financial markets has shown, the market will inevitably regress into a closed speculative loop. In losing a sense of measure, the financial markets lost contact with reality – and reality took revenge.

The introduction of the doctrine of 'New Public Management', with its system of indicators, transforms this loss of contact with reality from a risk into an inevitability, since it treats countries as though they were

---

11   A. Desrosières, *Pour une sociologie historique de la quantification*, vol. 1: *L'argument statistique*, 78.
12   Cit. D. Boyle, *The Tyranny of Numbers*, London: HarperCollins, 2000, 38.

businesses operating on a competitive market. States are to react to quantified signals supposed to constitute a true reflection of the world in which they operate, on the model of market prices. In the name of 'governance', this doctrine has had enormous influence on the reforms adopted over the past decade in the public sector. Unlike the statistical categories developed since Quételet, the new indicators used in governance do not simply aim to shed light on the implementation of public policy and the work of public bodies, but also to programme these by setting targets to improve performance with respect to competitors.[13] In the private sector, this development has radically transformed the meaning of accounting standards, which were previously used to remind companies of their responsibilities but are now used to benchmark their financial results.[14] Figures are not simply the framework in which an action takes place but, in this conception of governance drawn from cybernetics, they are its goal. Or rather, since neither public nor private operators are any longer supposed to execute *actions*, scores function as triggers for *re-action*, with a view to improving performance.

These public policy indicators are rooted in the same dogmas as those of Soviet planning, and they produce the same effects: public policy is driven by quantitative targets rather than concrete results,[15] and the real situation of the economy and society[16] is concealed from

---

13 See R. Salais, 'Capacités, base informationnelle et démocratie deliberative', in J. De Munck and B. Zimmermann, *La liberté au prisme des capacités*, Paris: EHESS, 2008, 297ff.

14 S. Jubé, *Droit social et normalisation compatable*, Paris: LGDJ lextenso, 2011.

15 This effect is well documented in the management sciences. See, among others, the case study on the effects of the Relative Cost Index, which is designed to measure the cost of hospital 'products', in J.-Cl. Moisdon (ed.), *Du mode d'existence des outils de gestion*, Paris: Seli Arslan, 1997, 114ff.

16 On the fallacies generated by reliance on individual performance

the ruling elites, who are totally disconnected from the lives of those they govern. The quantified representations of the world, which today determine how public and private affairs are run, imprison international organisations, states and businesses alike in an autistic universe of figures, which increasingly cuts them off from the reality of people's lives. One cannot judge reality without referring to a system of values lying outside it; and by the same token, one cannot challenge a system of values without first acknowledging that it is not a fact of nature, and can therefore be debated and contested. If one treats systems of values as quantifiable objects, one will make the measuring instruments give false readings and claim a scientific objectivity for one's system of values which it cannot possibly possess.

In this light, the indicators devised by the European Union or the World Bank to measure the performance of national legal systems epitomise the refusal to acknowledge the inherent normativity of such instruments. Not only are they not subjected to the stringencies of democratic debate, which is always a requirement in the legislative process, but the quantified images they provide do not reflect reality but rather the beliefs which inform their construction. Robert Salais has shown, for example, that in the attempt to improve ratings for immediate return to work, in the context of the Open Method of Coordination, it was necessary to behave as though the effects on the labour market of the increasing casualisation of employment were negligible. Since these indicators are based not on people's capacities but on the notion of employability, they also leave entirely out of account the effects on workers of the threat of losing their jobs, and they do not register what happens to the workers who do get a

---

indicators, see Chr. Dejours, *L'évaluation du travail à l'épreuve du réel. Critique des fondements de l'évaluation*, Dijon: INRA, 2003.

job, nor the nature of such jobs. Lastly, these indicators only start monitoring people once they have come onto the job market, and are therefore blind to everything which, before that stage, might prevent unemployment.[17]

The great Soviet writer and dissident (and logician) Alexander Zinoviev coined the phrase 'truthful lie' for this. A good example of such a lie is provided by the university system, after the introduction of ratings to determine bonuses and subsidies on the basis of the number of theses passed or the student failure rate at the end of the first few years. How best to comply? Nothing simpler than to lower standards.[18] Now that these types of performance indicators are also used to evaluate researchers (in terms of their 'citation index',[19] 'number of patents' or 'number of publications in refereed journals'), the pages Zinoviev devotes to research planning in the USSR (called 'Ibansk' in the book) is nothing less than prophetic:

We had forgotten research. We set about remedying that omission. A special meeting was called. We took the decision to enhance, improve and rectify. Then we came to concrete measures: 1) increase the number of students with doctorates, and doctors of science; 2) improve the way researchers are trained and the

17   See R. Salais, 'La politique des indicateurs. Du taux de chômage au taux d'emploi dans la Stratégie européenne pour l'emploi', in B. Zimmerman (ed.), *Les sciences sociales à l'épreuve de l'action: le savant, le politique et l'Europe*, Paris: Maison des sciences de l'Homme, 2004, 287–331.

18   See, for the case of Great Britain, M. Power, 'Research Evaluation in the Audit Society', in H. Matthies and D. Simon (eds.), *Wissenschaft unter Beobachtung. Effekte und Defekte von Evaluationen*, Wiesbaden: Verlag für Sozialwissenschaften, 2008, 15–24.

19   A 'citation index' is a quantifiable measure of a researcher's 'production', based on the number of references to his or her works in a certain number of journals.

theoretical and academic standard of theses; increase
the number of publications on current scientific
topics, etc. No sooner said than done. No hanging
around, as one says! And six months later the number
of doctorate holders had increased a hundredfold, and
doctors of science by ninety-nine. The total weight of
publications came to 100 million tonnes. It's no good
skimping on this kind of thing. You've got to think big.
And soon Ibansk was full to bursting with erudition.[20]

'Governance by numbers' is based on the belief that the
objects statistical categories are supposed to represent
actually exist in reality, and that the conventions of
equivalence which ground these categories can be dis-
counted. This mode of governance is therefore
particularly vulnerable to the pitfalls of self-reference,
as described by mathematical logic and particularly by
Russell and Whitehead more than a century ago, in
their theory of types,[21] which was developed in order to
solve logical paradoxes (such as 'What I am saying
now is untrue'). Gödel took issue with certain aspects
of this theory, but his mathematical demonstrations of
the principle of incompletion basically corroborate it,
particularly its core thesis that no totality can belong
to itself or presuppose itself.[22] And this principle
applies no less to human societies than to the human
mind.

Russell's theory of types puts into particularly
sharp relief the logical function of inter-diction. It

---

20   A. Zinoviev, *The Yawning Heights*, trans. Gordon Clough, New
York: Random House, 1979.

21   First described in an article by Bertrand Russell in 1908 and later
developed with A.N. Whitehead in the first volume of their *Principia
Mathematica*, Cambridge: Cambridge University Press, 1910.

22   On Gödel's theorem and its implications, see R. Penrose, *The
Emperor's New Mind: Concerning Computers, Minds, and the Laws of
Physics*, Oxford and New York: Oxford University Press, 1989; see also
P. Cassou-Noguès, *Gödel*, Paris: Les Belles Lettres, 2004.

shows that self-referential (autopoietic?) thought is unsustainable, and that every normative statement of type *n* must be referred to a type at level *n+1*, if the principle of non-contradiction is to be respected. One can understand in this light why Norbert Wiener, one of the fathers of cybernetics, devoted his last work to 'Certain Points where Cybernetics Impinges on Religion'.[23] Wiener was a scholar and not a scientist. He understood that the dogmatic question of inter-diction could not be dismissed without thereby destroying the very foundations of human rationality. Inter-diction is what enables people to talk to rather than to kill each other. Eradicating all inter-dictions in the name of economic freedom will inevitably lead to the strong crushing the weak and violence taking hold. This is why reviving the spirit of Philadelphia is an urgent task. In this domain as in others, reconnecting with a tradition does not mean blocking the movement of history, but quite the opposite. It means using the insights of the past to understand the present and imagine the future. The problem is not restoring the conditions that prevailed before the neo-liberal revolution, but envisaging the concrete forms that social justice must take today.

23 N. Wiener, 'A Comment on Certain Points where Cybernetics Impinges on Religion', in *God & Golem, Inc.*, Cambridge, Mass.: MIT Press, 1964.

PART II

Achieving Social Justice Today

The meltdown of the financial markets in autumn 2008 is only the surface sign of a deeper crisis, which is basically a crisis of law. To understand this, we must recall that for markets to function effectively, they must operate within a three-dimensional world in which relations between economic operators are placed under the aegis of a third entity which guarantees equitable exchange over the longer term of human life. If we set foot in any medieval marketplace – for example, the *Marktplatz* in Brussels, where the magnificent architecture of the buildings bordering the square highlights their symbolic role in ensuring the market's reliability – we find the town hall, symbol of the public authorities, which vouch for fair exchange (compliance with the legal standards of weights and measures) and the houses of the guilds (butchers, bakers, brewers, etc.), which guarantee the status and quality of the work of each trade, without which there is no created wealth to exchange. These buildings also mark the outer limits of the market. If we leave this space to go to the law courts or the royal palace, for example, we are immediately subject to other rules, for if market rules applied to legal or political decisions, they could be bought and sold, and the *polis* would degenerate into a corrupt organisation in which honest merchants could no longer freely go about their business.

Today's markets may not have this same geographical and architectural unity, but they continue to operate under the same sets of conditions. For example, a valid contract can be formed between two parties only if a guarantor (the gods, the monarch, the state, and so forth) oversees their pledge. Failing this, a contract is nothing more than the law of the strongest. Likewise, the right to property is not a binary relation between a person and a thing, since, once again, it is a genuine right only when a third party can guarantee that the property of each is respected by all.[24] When this condition is not met, for example if the state is weak or corrupt, the fiction of a legal bond between a thing and a person – and one person exclusively – is no longer tenable. Relations of dependence govern people's lives once more, and the weak are obliged to curry favour with the strong in order to come out of it alive and not be stripped of what few possessions they have.

In other words, global markets are embedded within sets of institutional relations which thirty years of neo-liberalism and communist market economies have done their utmost to destroy, by deregulating the financial markets and introducing competition between national systems of welfare and environmental protection. It was foreseeable, from a purely legal point of view, that the financial markets, where deregulation had been pushed the furthest, would be the first to collapse. But it was also foreseeable from an economic point of view and had long been predicted by certain economists – those who do not necessarily publish in

---

24 See A. Macfarlane, 'The Mystery of Property: Inheritance and Industrialization in England and Japan', in C.M. Hann (ed.), *Property Relations: Renewing the Anthropological Tradition*, Cambridge: Cambridge University Press, 1998, 104ff.

'peer-reviewed journals' and to whom no one would dream of awarding a prize 'in memory of Alfred Nobel', the Nobel Prize in Economics.[25]

We should not be surprised that these legal and economic warnings have gone unheeded (and a similar fate most probably awaits the deregulation of welfare and environmental protection). This is because, while legal dogma is conscious of its status and open to reinterpretation, scientistic thought does not acknowledge its dogmatic basis and is utterly impervious to any sort of external critique. That is its strength, but also its weakness when, as is happening today, neo-liberal doctrine is overtaken by the reality principle, and the economic and political elites which embody it prove incapable of understanding why their world is falling apart around their ears. We are already familiar with this scenario from the time when socialists and communists, in their inability to think through the decay or collapse of 'scientific socialism', shifted within the space of a few years from unconditionally defending it to unconditionally rallying to the new neo-liberal credo. And this phenomenon has reappeared with the people – often the same ones – who supported neo-liberalism and who got to where they are now thanks to it.

The most fundamental belief they hold is that 'the market' makes the world go round, as the latter's supreme regulatory instance, and that it must have the last word on how companies, and the political economy of countries all over the globe, are run. In view of this, it is hardly surprising that the measures taken by the

---

25   See in particular, for France, the work by Jean-Luc Gréau published more than ten years ago under the unambiguous title of *Le capitalisme malade de sa finance* [Capitalism's Financial System Makes It Ill], Paris: Gallimard, 1998; or the more recent warnings of François Morin in *Le nouveau mur de l'argent: Essai sur la finance globalisée*, Paris: Seuil, 2006.

neo-liberals to restart the economy in the face of the collapse of the financial markets should take the form of flooding them with public money, rather than examining the structural causes of their collapse. What we are witnessing is pyromaniac firefighters dousing with petrol the engine they had set alight in the hope this will kick-start it. At most, the neo-liberals concede that these markets should be better regulated, but since they continue to treat rules like products competing on an international market of norms, they are still trapped within the self-referential circle created by the belief that the market can regulate the market.

However, the challenge is not to adjust market mechanisms in the way one might adjust one's central heating.[26] It is, rather, to bring the markets back into the arena of legal and political debate, so that a proper hierarchy of means and ends between economic and financial fields on the one hand, and people's needs on the other, can be re-established. In other words, it is a question of reviving the spirit of the Declaration of Philadelphia, which drew on the lessons of the Second World War, and in which the economic and financial spheres are subordinated to the imperatives of human dignity and social justice. This does not mean reverting to the modes of social and political organisation institutionalised in the post-war boom years. Although the socio-economic achievements of the post-war period are certainly much more impressive than those of the ensuing thirty years of neo-liberalism, that is no longer our world. The definition of social justice adopted by the Declaration of Philadelphia in 1944, by contrast, has not aged in the slightest, which is why the ILO's 'Declaration on Social Justice for a Fair Globalization'

---

26   A. Supiot, 'Governing Work and Welfare in a Global Economy', in J. Zeitling and D. Trubet (eds.), *Governing Work and Welfare in a New Economy: European and American Experiments*, Oxford: Oxford University Press, 2003, 376–406

(2008) simply refers back to it. The Declaration of Philadelphia helps us realise that the paths we forge for the future must measure up to the demands of the present. We must therefore leave the flat and horizon-less world of neo-liberal dogma, and regain the use of our 'five senses', which have been seriously blunted by thirty years of structural adjustment of human needs to the prescriptions of the financial sector. These 'five senses' are the sense of limits, of measure, of action, of responsibility and of solidarity.

5

THE ART OF LIMITS

Central to the notion of a legal system is that the laws comprising it are entirely manmade, and hence can have no absolute value. The democratic ideal is for each people to decide on the laws best suited to its geographical and cultural context. This territorial inscription of laws has, for the last two centuries, produced a mosaic of sovereign states, where each is conceived as an immortal being whose physical body is renewed at every generation. The generations are bound together through their common belonging to the same people, whose survival and prosperity the state has the duty to guarantee across the centuries. The very first sentence of the Constitution of the United States of America is an admirable summary of this metaphysical construction: 'We the People of the United States, in Order to form a more perfect Union, establish Justice, insure domestic Tranquillity, provide for the common defence, promote the general Welfare, and secure the Blessings of Liberty to ourselves and our Posterity, do ordain and establish this Constitution for the United States of America.' After decolonisation, this type of organisation was generalised across the globe, and states became the frameworks within which the rule of law could be established, without which 'man is . . .

compelled to have recourse, as a last resort, to rebellion against tyranny and oppression' (Universal Declaration of Human Rights). In other words, the rule of law accommodates a diversity of territories in which a diversity of laws are in force. Each person is allocated a place fit to inhabit, and each must respect the place of others. By 'place', we mean first and foremost an identity, which cannot be arbitrarily annulled and which is assigned to each person prior to his or her appearance as a free subject on the scene of exchange. In secular societies, where the legal system is divorced from religion, it is the *state* which certifies every person's identity by reference to a filiation and a territory, and in so doing attributes him or her a civil *status*.

THE PRIVATISATION OF LAWS

Today, the abolition of all barriers which might hinder the free circulation of goods and capital across the globe seriously compromises the territorial anchorage of laws.[1] Countries are no longer able to ensure that their national legislation holds sway within their territories. This situation strikes at the heart of national solidarity systems, since it encourages tax havens with lower welfare contributions. It allows the richest to exploit the technique of legal personality in the same way that gangsters go hooded to avoid being recognised, and so escape the justice system. Where the Total Market prevails, money has the last word on defining where we belong, and any qualitative differences between people or between things, or even – as the human body itself is treated as an asset – between people and things, is to be superseded.

Logically enough, in a world managed like a set of quantifiable resources, difference can be envisaged only

---

1 See my 'L'inscription territoriale des lois', 151–70.

as discrimination, and equality only as indifference. For the neo-liberal right, the economy is the field in which all differences other than financial ones are to be abolished; their targets are consequently the public services and employment protection measures. For the left, it is civil and familial status which must give way to the 'free choice' of a flexible identity, by eradicating sexual and generational differences.[2] In both cases, insecurity, flexibility and an uncertain future are treated as life-giving principles. This was precisely the message which came across loud and clear from the rhetorical question posed by the head of the French national employers' movement, the MEDEF: 'Life, health and love are precarious – so why should work be any different?'[3]

In response to the erosion of the foundations of people's identity in personal and professional life, the most varied forms of nationalism and particularism resurface. Those who feel the socio-political ground giving way beneath their feet seek firmer territory elsewhere, and turn zealously to religion, skin colour, gender or sexual orientation, commemorating the history of their victimhood or laying claim to indigenous status in any of its myriad forms, for which roots are invented at will. This rise in identity claims eclipses the socio-economic causes of social injustice.[4] Thus

2   One of the priorities of the French left today is to recognise the 'right to adapt one's civil status to one's gender'; see 'Refusons la transphobie, respectons l'identité de genre!' [No to Transphobia, Yes to Recognition of Gender Identity!], *Le Monde*, 16 May 2009.

In 1932, Jünger had already noted that since liberalism attempts to transform every relation into a contractual bond which can be annulled, one of its ideals is 'quite logically' attained 'when an individual can cancel his sexual character, and determine or change it simply by going down to the registry office' (Jünger, *Der Arbeiter*).

3   *Le Figaro économie*, 30 Aug. 2005.

4   R. Castel, *La discrimination négative. Citoyens ou indigènes?*, Paris: Seuil, 2007.

the primary cause of 'inner-city problems' is not poverty, unemployment and the lack of public services there, but the 'origins' of the inhabitants, by which we are to understand their religion or skin colour. Considerations of race, belief and gender were deemed irrelevant for a definition of social justice in the 1944 Declaration, but today there is a whole current of thought which envisages justice precisely in terms of recognition of such particularities.[5]

The terms in which justice is conceived shift here from having to being, from the realm of the socio-economic to that of identity. The 'right to difference' is championed by minority groups – ethnic, sexual or religious – who appeal to religious freedom or to their position as victims in order to win special status and hence limit the scope of the law applicable to all inhabitants of the same territory.[6] As for the individual, the inalienability of civil status is challenged by the right to privacy, with the claim that each person should be able to decide on his or her own identity.[7] This shift from the territoriality of laws to their privatisation, in its

5   C. Taylor, *Multiculturalism and 'The Politics of Recognition'*, Princeton: Princeton University Press, 1992; A. Honneth, *The Struggle for Recognition: The Moral Grammar of Social Conflicts*, trans. Joel Anderson, Cambridge: Polity Press, 1995; N. Fraser, *Adding Insult to Injury: Social Justice and the Politics of Recognition*, ed. Kevin Olson, London: Verso, 1999.

6   For the United States, see M. Piore, *Beyond Individualism*, Cambridge, Mass.: Harvard University Press, 1995, 215; for Canada, see A. Lajoie, *Quand les minorités font la loi*, Paris: PUF, 2002, 217.

7   For this shift towards a self-determined personal status in the name of the right to privacy, see H. Muir Watt, *Droit international privé* 2: 642, 43ff.; D. Gutman, *Le sentiment d'identité. Étude de droit des personnes et de la famille*, Paris: LGDJ, 2000, 340ff.; and J.-L. Ranchon, 'Indisponibilité, ordre public et autonomie de la volonté dans le droit des personnes et de la famille', in A. Wijffels (ed.), *Le code civil entre ius commune et droit privé européen*, Brussels: Bruylant, 2005, 269ff.

individualist form of 'a law for me' and 'myself as law',
is the legal expression of the narcissism characterising
this latest stage in Western culture.[8] For example, the
European Court of Human Rights now champions 'the
right to establish details of their [individuals'] identity
as individual human beings'.[9] In many respects, Islamic
fundamentalism is nothing but a reflection of this narcissism, as suggested by what is called *fatwamania* in
Sunni countries, and the fact that any imam can claim
to lay down the law.[10] This narcissism is destructive
because it forces us into the situation described by
Pierre Legendre: 'No liberation awaits the subject
forced to act as Third towards himself. On the contrary, it is a crushing burden when social relations are
transformed *politically* into a free-for-all under the
veneer of a discourse of generalised seduction. What is
implied by the new legal forms inspired by managerial
practices is clear for all to see, and I would summarise
it as follows: *good luck to you*.'[11]

Identity-based claims and the rejection of one's roots
are in the last instance two sides of the same coin,
namely the difficulty of ensuring that each of us feels
sufficiently secure to be able to act and move freely.
The removal of all barriers which might obstruct the
free circulation of goods and capital goes hand in hand
with the erection of barriers to prevent the free

8 C. Lasch, *Culture of Narcissism: American Life in an Age of
Diminishing Expectations*, New York: Norton, 1979.
9 ECHR, 11 July 2002, *Christine Goodwin v. The United Kingdom*,
application no. 28957/95.
10 See Y. Habib, 'Halal, haram, sport panarabe', *Le Temps* (Algiers),
19 Sept. 2008.
11 'Infliger au sujet d'être pour lui-même le Tiers, c'est non pas le
libérer, mais l'écraser, transformer *politiquement* les relations sociales
en foire d'empoigne, sous le masque d'un discours de séduction
généralisé. L'implicite des nouvelles légalités de facture gestionnaire
peut être mis à découvert et je le résumerai ainsi: *survive qui pourra*.' P.
Legendre, *Les enfants du Texte. Étude sur la fonction parentale des
États*, Paris: Fayard, 1992, 352.

circulation of human beings, precisely those who are plunged into poverty and driven into exile by their removal in the first place. It is clear, then, that globalisation oscillates between the utopia of a world which has become fluid and without frontiers, and the multiplication of barriers and gated communities. Faced with such an alternative, we should avoid the temptation both of reinstating the limits we had in the past, and of behaving as though they had never existed and there could be a tabula rasa. We must start by accepting that the figure of the sovereign, which has governed our representations of the state and the individual since the beginning of modern times, has had its day.

THE RETURN OF FEUDALISM

The concept of sovereignty has been the lynchpin of the theory of the state since the sixteenth century,[12] but it is incapable of making sense of the state's contemporary transformations. Although authors who discuss its decline tend to use the metaphor of the pyramid and the network,[13] we should not overlook the fact that networks are a feudal invention. This should alert us to the fact that the law being developed today in the context of globalisation is informed by previous legal forms. The networked society does not imply the victory of contract over law or 'civil society' over the state, but rather the re-emergence of socio-political forms which predate the sovereign state. This should come as no

12   J. Bodin, *Six Books of the Commonwealth*, Oxford: Basil Blackwell, 1967.
13   See M. Castells, *The Rise of the Network Society*, Cambridge, Mass. and Oxford: Blackwell, 1996; F. Ost and M. van de Kerchove, *De la pyramide au réseau? Pour une théorie dialectique du droit*, Brussels: Presses universitaires de Saint-Louis, 2002; G. Teubner, *Networks as Connected Contracts*, trans. Michelle Everson, ed. and intro. Hugh Collins, Oxford: Hart, 2011.

surprise: as Aziz Al Azmeh has shown for Islam,[14] or Pierre Legendre for the West, the dogmatic categories of the past do not fit neatly into a linear history but constitute a reservoir of sense which can always reappear and produce new normative effects. One of the reasons why legal dogma accumulates like a sediment is that there are a finite number of types of legal structure, and only variations within each type are affected by historical change.

Borrowing from Chinese political philosophy, one can distinguish broadly between two systems of government: government by laws and government by men. In a system of government by laws, the law expresses the will of a sovereign power and applies to all equally; that all should be subject to general and abstract laws is the condition of freedom for each. This structure supposes the presence of a *third*, who is both source and guarantor of laws, and who transcends the will and interests of individuals. Two distinct legal planes are articulated in this dogmatic configuration: the calculable and the incalculable. The latter concerns issues (above all those of civil status) which transcend any calculation of individual utility, and belong to the realm of deliberation and the law. The former concerns whatever falls within the realm of the calculation of individual utility and therefore within that of negotiation and contract. It is what allows men and things to be treated as abstract entities which can be exchanged, and whose value can be determined by a shared monetary standard. Their qualitative differences, meanwhile, are enshrined in the domain of the law and the incalculable.

In a system of government by men, on the other

14   A. Al Azmeh, 'Chronophagous Discourse: A Study of Clerico-Legal Appropriation of the World in an Islamic Tradition', in F.E. Reynolds and D. Tracy (eds.), *Religion and Practical Reason*, Albany: State University of New York Press, 1994, 163ff.

hand, each person is placed within a network of relations of dependence. The guiding idea is not that all should be subject to the same abstract law, but that each person should behave in accordance with his or her place in the network. Each must serve the interests of those on whom he depends, and be able to count on the loyalty of those who are dependent on him. The legal status of people, their relations to others as well as to things, is defined in terms of these networks of personal bonds, not in terms of subjection to the same impersonal law. This type of configuration blurs the distinction between the calculable and the incalculable, since laws are the outcome of negotiation between representatives of different interest groups, and at the same time issues of general interest spill over into the contractual sphere. The figure of the third as guarantor does not disappear altogether, but fragments into a multiplicity of poles linked to each other within the same network. Consequently, the position of the state looks less and less like *sovereignty* and increasingly like *suzerainty*.[15]

The return of suzerainty at a national level is apparent in the contracting-out of public projects. As the welfare state struggles under an impossible number of responsibilities, its tasks are increasingly managed by private operators who are in turn supervised by independent authorities the state has set up and nominated.[16] Such techniques of regulation[17] reintroduce the figure of the

15 Whereas the sovereign holds supreme power, which can be exercised directly over all his subjects, the suzerain's power can be exercised directly only over his vassals and not over his vassals' vassals; see J.-F. Lemarignier, *La France médiévale. Institutions et société*, Paris: A. Colin, 1970, 256ff.

16 See the French Council of State's reports, *Les autorités administratives indépendantes* (2001) and *Le contrat, mode d'action publique et de production de normes* (2008).

17 See M.-A. Frison-Roche, *Règles et pouvoirs dans les systèmes de régulation*, Paris: Dalloz, 2004.

suzerain, whose power over his subjects is only indirect, and also the old distinction between power and
authority, which characterises how feudalism binds
powers in order to avoid the concentration of power in
too few hands.

This revival of feudal bonds is most visible in
European law. The supreme power presiding over
European institutions is clearly not a sovereign
power. The EU directives destined for member states
should not be confused with laws, whatever the mis-
understandings generated on this issue by the Draft
Treaty establishing a Constitution for Europe. If
there is one defining characteristic of this legal order,
it is that it transforms member states into vassals of
a European Union which is itself deprived of most of
the attributes of sovereignty over its citizens. In other
words, the supreme authority in Europe has only
indirect power over its own populations and requires
the mediation of its member states, in the same way
the human body requires its limbs. Likewise for
certain international economic organisations such as
the IMF, whose (generally destructive) power over
people's lives can only be exercised through the
allegiance of states which accept its structural adjustment programmes in return for a portion of their
sovereignty. These programmes are not based on
contractual obligation but on an act of allegiance,
formalised in a letter addressed by the country concerned to the IMF.[18]

This return of 'government by men' also affects
issues of personal status. Descartes' figure of the individual freed from any bonds could develop only in the
context of a sovereign state (Descartes' *cogito* comes
forty years after Bodin's theory of sovereignty). It could
thrive only where personal status was decided by

18   These letters are published on the IMF's website, imf.org/external/
index.htm.

general and abstract laws equally applicable to all. By contrast, when a person's condition depends on his or her position in a network of contractual ties, however densely or loosely woven they are, the autonomy of the will inevitably suffers. We have examples of this when a sovereign state collapses or becomes corrupt, shattering the illusion of an individual's sovereignty, as people find themselves obliged to swear allegiance to those more powerful than themselves for even a minimum of security and freedom. A situation common in traditional societies then re-emerges, where the number of people on whom a person can depend is a measure of their importance.

This shift from law to allegiance characterises the plethora of new contracts which not only oblige the parties to give, do, or not do something specific, but also create between them a bond which obliges one party to behave according to the expectations of the other. This type of contract is used increasingly frequently to reintegrate into the workforce people threatened with, or victims of, exclusion. More generally, it is used when one person seeks to involve another in his or her economic activity. The contract affects the employment status of the two parties and obliges them to create more or less stable bonds between them. Company and distribution law in their entirety illustrate this trend, as does the exponential increase in the number of techniques for creating subsidiaries, subcontracting, outsourcing and so forth. The expression 'contractual solidarity' (*solidarisme contractuel*), which is sometimes applied to these developments,[19] sounds appealing but is actually misleading, since it

---

19 See D. Mazeaud, 'Loyauté, solidarité, fraternité: la nouvelle devise contractuelle?', in *L'avenir du droit. Mélanges en hommage à François Terré*, Paris: PUF, 1999, 603ff.; and Chr. Jamin, 'Plaidoyer pour le solidarisme contractuel', in *Études offertes à J.Ghestin*, Paris: LGDJ, 441.

disregards the precise legal meaning which 'solidarity' has acquired in social law. It would be more accurate to talk of techniques of enfeoffment, of tenure-services, which enable a business concern to be franchised on condition that the operator agrees to a certain number of controls by the franchisor, and in return the franchisor ensures that the business remains economically viable within certain limits. Among other things, this leads to the re-emergence of an issue that modern economics thought was dead and buried, the issue of 'just price'.[20]

THE LIMITS OF DEPENDENCE

It is futile to deplore these developments, and illusory to think one could simply restore the power of nation states and government by laws. The emergence of a new condition of generalised dependence is the legal system's allergic response to the madness of what Pierre Legendre calls 'the auto-founded Subject King'. The suffering palpable everywhere in our hyper-modern societies is caused by the fact that we are all exhorted to run our lives as though we had sovereign autonomy, while at the same time who we are is not secured by law but is in fact dependent on the strength of the emotional and economic bonds we have managed to form with others. This puts us on a straight path to narcissism or depression, and it is a trend we should not ignore. If we can curb it, we might be able to rid ourselves of the destructive utopian beliefs which

---

20   Price-fixing is punishable by law if the price is not fixed by contract (*Cour de cassation*, Plenary Session, 1 Dec. 1995, *Bulletin civil 9*, 1995). See M. Frison-Roche, 'De l'abandon du carcan de l'indétermination à l'abus dans la fixation du prix', *Revue de jurisprudence de droit des affaires* 3, 1996; M. Fabre-Magnan, *Contrat et engagement unilatéral*, Paris: PUF, 2008, 356ff. Also see A. de Senarclens, 'La maxime "pretium debet esse verum, certum, justum"', *Mélanges Paul Fournier*, Paris: Sirey, 1929, 685.

globalisation brings in its wake. The feudal bonds which are resurfacing today can take us in two directions: towards a mafia organisation or towards a state of partial dependence, in which fundamental rights and freedoms would continue to be secured. All depends on our ability to define new limits appropriate to the present state of the world.

The art of limits plays the same role for legal systems as do doors and windows in architecture, offering protection, but also opening onto the outside. Limits are neither walls nor sieves, and they must protect us both from the ideal of a world without borders and from the real threat of a world where everyone lives behind closed doors. At the international level, rediscovering a sense of limits would lead us to contain international trade within new frontiers, so that it furthers the interests of social justice. We urgently need to re-establish a robust socio-political matrix for the market economy, so that competition may exist between companies and not legal systems. There is no market without limits fixed by law. The European Community sought to extend and not destroy what was still called the 'internal market', and it drew on its experience of industrialisation, when European countries fixed the legal conditions for prosperity by opening their frontiers only insofar as was economically beneficial. The market – the cornerstone of the European Community – was 'common' insofar as it was based both on competition between companies and on solidarity between countries. But this vision was doomed from the moment member states and the Commission backed the idea of a total market in which any obstacle to the free circulation of goods and capital, in whatever sector or country it existed, was targeted for destruction. This unchecked extension of the market inevitably destroyed solidarity between member states and introduced competition between their national legal systems.

The free circulation of goods and capital is not an end in itself, and it is only of value if it really helps improve people's lives. It is for the law to extend or restrict the free market, depending on whether the latter enriches people's working lives and protects them from poverty, or whether on the contrary it deprives people of work and plunges them into poverty. This principle, to which the first industrial powers owed their success, is the same one to have enabled China and India to emerge as new economic powers. Why should it not be applied to Africa or Europe today? Controlling the circulation of goods between these huge markets would encourage long-term investment, since companies could be confident that all competitors were playing by the same rules. And opportunistic and volatile investments which aim at re-importing onto a home market products whose conditions of manufacture have infringed the social and environmental rules in force on home ground would be less attractive.[21]

Other avenues could also usefully be explored, namely in corporation law. Until recently, the Netherlands had a law restricting a company's board members to those shareholders who had proved their commitment to the company's long-term interests. This law upheld the traditional conception of the business enterprise in continental Europe,[22] in that it distinguished between two types of shareholders – those interested in the long-term success of the business, and those seeking to make the greatest short-term gains, who can be as dangerous for a company as a swarm of locusts for a farm crop. The first type of shareholder accepts the principle

21 On the return of a moderate form of protectionism, organised around large continental blocs, see J.-L. Gréau, *L'avenir du capitalisme*, Paris: Gallimard, 2005, 212ff.
22 See D. Kalff, *An Unamerican Business: The Rise of the New European Enterprise*, London: Kogan Page Ltd, 2005, 224.

of the company's legal autonomy, while the second behaves as though it were the company's owners (which is not legally the case). Clearly, the weighting given in corporation law to one or the other type of shareholder will have a much greater impact on employment levels than will the degree of protection provided by redundancy legislation. If new limits were set on the power of shareholders, such that they could no longer disregard the long-term health of the company in which they are investing, then business entrepreneurship could regain the leading role in a country's economy that it should never have lost in the first place.

Lastly, the courts too must preserve – or rediscover – a sense of limits. Their power has grown in proportion to the decline in the power of nation states. For example, as regards the European judiciary, were the highest jurisdictions of member states to realise that the European Court of Justice does not have sovereign power, but rather the position of a suzerain, they might summon up the courage to resist its rulings whenever it oversteps the role assigned to it on paper and behaves as though it had sovereign jurisdiction. The Cour de cassation in France or the Bundesarbeitsgericht in Germany could, for example, claim that outlawing strike action, as decided by the European Court in the *Laval* and *Viking* cases (see chapter 3), falls outside the competence of the Court as defined in the European Treaty, that it contravenes French legislation on the right to strike and also ILO norms regarding freedom of association, and that consequently these rulings should not be transposed into national legislation.

The German Constitutional Court was the first to show that national jurisdictions were alive to this issue. It examined the provisions of the Treaty of Lisbon in great detail and concluded that due to the 'structural deficit in democratic legitimacy' of the European

Union, the ratification of this Treaty would have to be predicated on passing a law to 'guarantee the efficacy of [German citizens'] voting rights' and to ensure that the EU 'does not exceed the competences granted it'.[23]

23   See the Court's website, bundesverfassungsgericht.de, decision no. 72/2009 of 30 June 2009. This major decision was hardly mentioned in the French media, and never seriously analysed. See the English-language special supplement devoted to it by the *German Law Journal* 10: 8, 2009, at germanlawjournal.com.

6

A SENSE OF MEASURE

We do not need to go back as far as Aristotle to appreciate that the practice of justice requires a sense of measure.[1] Since law, in the words of the most venerable *Digest*, is 'the art of discovering the good and the equal' (*Jus est ars boni et æqui*), and justice 'the constant and perpetual will to render to every man his due' (*Justitia est constans et perpetua voluntas jus suum cuique tribuendi*), their practice requires that what each person is owed be measured. Keeping a sense of measure means defining a golden mean between what is 'too much' and what is 'not enough', which in turn supposes that one has both a precise *representation* of the facts and the capacity to *evaluate* them – that is, to link them to a system of values. Every measurement has these cognitive and normative aspects, but legal rules, unlike mathematical or religious norms, are not inviolable and must be reworked in the light of lacks or excesses. As such, preserving a sense of measure means always setting the definition of what *should be* alongside the knowledge of what *is*.

We are obliged to recall these basic facts in order to combat the seductive mirage of quantification. Today's

---

1 See Aristotle, *Nicomachean Ethics*, bk V, chap. 6. See also M. Villey, *Le droit et les droits de l'homme*, Paris: PUF, 1983, 52ff.

pipe dream is governance by numbers, by which we hope to circumvent the need to understand and compare situations, and so be spared the trouble of judging and therefore of thinking. But this dream has the makings of a nightmare. Claiming to 'evaluate' the quality of a piece of work by using performance indicators divorced from the singular experience of *doing* that work is at once destructive, unrealistic and conducive to illness.[2] Decreeing that the way in which the 'spontaneous order of the market' distributes wealth is fair creates massive, and unjustifiable, inequalities.[3] And modifying public policy in order to conform to the macroeconomic indicators to which one attributes universal validity is nothing more than a fetishism of the sign, which divorces leaders from the people and things they are meant to govern.[4]

The process whereby units of measurement gradually became divorced from any human experience is historically linked to the progress of modern science and the advent of capitalism. General and abstract units of measurement like the metre (defined since 1983 as the length travelled by light in a vacuum for the duration of 1/299792458 of a second) gradually displaced the foot, span, league and bushel, which measured all sorts of things in relation to the human body or the inherent qualities of the object measured.[5]

---

2 See Chr. Dejours, *L'évaluation du travail à l'épreuve du réel: Critique des fondements de l'évaluation*, Dijon: INRA, 2003.

3 See the damning assessment by the International Labour Organisation in its *World of Work Report 2008: Income Inequalities in the Age of Financial Globalization*, Geneva: International Labour Office, 2008, available for download at ilo.org/public/english/bureau/inst/download/world08.pdf.

4 See R. Salais, 'Usages et mésusages de l'argument statistique: le pilotage des politiques publiques par la performance', *Revue Française des Affaires Sociales*, 2009.

5 See F. Jedrzejewski, *Histoire universelle de la mesure*, Paris: Ellipses, 2002.

The 'dehumanisation' of measurement is perfectly appropriate when observing and explaining natural phenomena such as the movement of the planets or the physics of sub-atomic particles. Its effects become questionable in any representation of the *oecumene*, that is, the human being's living environment.[6] When we measure land in hectares, for example, we lose sight of the fact that no one hectare is qualitatively the same as any other, which was precisely what 'archaic' land measurements such as the *furlong* or the *hide* took into account, whose size – correlated to the distance a plough team could be driven without rest or the amount of land able to support a single household for agricultural and taxation purposes – varied according to the quality of the land.[7] And when it is a question of attributing 'to each his own' and establishing a system of human justice, the dehumanisation of units of measurement removes us so far from reality that it can lead to sheer madness. In this domain, Protagoras' dictum 'Man is the measure of all things' is the only principle to have any sense.

In order to recover a sense of measure, we must place the fate of human beings back squarely in the centre of evaluations of economic performance. Two priorities contained in the Declaration of Philadelphia can guide us here. The first is social justice, which must once again become the unit of measurement by which to assess the adequacy of a legal order, such that 'all national and international policies and measures, in particular those of an economic and financial character, should be judged in this light and accepted only in so far as they may be held to promote and not to hinder the achievement of this fundamental

---

6 For these concepts, see A. Berque, *Écoumène. Introduction à l'étude des milieux humains*, Paris: Belin, 2000.
7 See W. Kula, *Les mesures et les hommes*, Paris: Éd. de la MSH, 1984, 38ff.

objective' (art. IIc). The second is the requisite of social democracy, so that evaluations take into account the widest possible range of situations, and 'the representatives of workers and employers' join 'in free discussion and democratic decision with a view to the promotion of the common welfare' (art. Id).

THE UNIT OF MEASURE: SOCIAL JUSTICE

Making progress in social justice the measure of successful economic performance is a simple and sensible idea, yet its adoption by the Declaration of Philadelphia was nothing short of revolutionary. True to its full title of 'Declaration Concerning the *Aims* and *Purposes* of the International Labour Organisation', the Declaration of Philadelphia conceived of law not only as a system of rules not to be transgressed, but also as a set of goals to be accomplished. The 'central aim of national and international policy' is to ensure respect for the right of all human beings 'to pursue both their material well-being and their spiritual development in conditions of freedom and dignity, of economic security and equal opportunity' (DePh, art II). In fact, there is nothing very surprising about considering a normative system as a set of paths to be followed; at the very root of the French term *le Droit* is the concept of *direction*, from the medieval Latin *directum*. Other great civilisations share this idea, for example in the Indian notion of *maryādā*, which designates a target to be reached but not overstepped – that is, at once the aim and the limit of an action.[8]

However, this teleological conception of a body of legal rules – one defined in terms of its goals – clashed head-on with Western positivist doctrine, which rejects any reference to the idea of Justice, and so ends up with

8   See C. Malamoud, 'Une perspective indienne sur la notion de dignité humaine', Conference, Nantes IAS, April 2009, forthcoming.

a 'science of law' reduced to a description of norms as bare mechanical parts. This explains the paradoxical fate of the notion of 'objectives', as introduced in the Declaration: on the one hand, the idea that countries should be bound by objectives, in the social field where the notion arose, was roundly criticised by conservative jurists, a cause soon taken up by the neo-liberals, who accused social law of being programmatic and hence a sham, lacking justiciability.[9] This had at least one major legal consequence for Europe, namely the exclusion of the majority of social rights from the Convention for the Protection of Human Rights and Fundamental Freedoms adopted in 1950, and their relegation, ten years later, to a document stripped of any real normative force, the Social Charter.

On the other hand, in the economic and financial spheres, the teleological conception of normativity caught on like wildfire. Not, of course, in order to measure the extent to which social justice had been achieved, but in order to force compliance with the 'spontaneous order' of the market. The structural adjustment programmes prescribed for poor countries by the IMF, the economic convergence criteria imposed on Eurozone members,[10] and the Broad Economic Policy Guidelines set by the European Council are some of the better-known examples of this type of normativity, which has as one of its explicit goals to prevent increases in work-related revenues (which would be inflationist), while supporting increases in revenue from capital (rebaptised 'value creation'). This goal-orientated normativity is also present in

9   There seems to be no lack of new choristers to chant this old tune; see, for example, J.-Ph. Feldman, 'Le comité de réflexion sur le Préambule de la Constitution et la philosophie des droits de l'homme', *Recueil Dalloz*, 2009, 1036.
10   *Consolidated Version of the Treaty Establishing the European Community*, art. 121, § 1. There are four quantifiable criteria: price stability, the sustainability of the government's financial position, exchange rates and long-term interest-rate levels.

the jurisprudence of the European Court of Justice, which has justified its deregulation of national bodies of legislation in the spheres of work, consumption, social protection, taxation and public services – to name but a few – precisely in terms of the goal of removing trade barriers.[11] A teleological normativity is employed here against its original purpose of ensuring the advance of social justice.

This double standard shows the flimsiness, if not the bad faith, of claiming the non-justiciability of the objectives of social justice. An objective is both a goal to be achieved and a limit not to be overstepped, and it always has the character of an obligation which can stand up in a court of law. One need only observe the tomes of Community case-law involving applicants successfully bringing actions on the grounds that national legislation has infringed European objectives of trade liberalisation to be convinced of this. If social justice were to be made one of the fundamental objectives of the European Union, nothing would prevent the Court of Justice from declaring contrary to that objective national legislation which, for example, encourages hours of work incompatible with a normal family and social life, such as the abolition of Sunday rest. This is exactly what the European Court of Human Rights has done. It draws its method of interpretation from the European Convention on Human Rights, which refers to 'the general principles of law recognised by civilised nations'. It incorporates all international and European labour norms, including those of the ILO and the European Charter of Fundamental Rights.[12] Given the principle of the indi-

---

11   See above, chap. 3.

12   ECHR (Grand Chamber), 12 Nov. 2008, *Demir and Baykara v. Turkey* (application no. 34503/97). See also ECHR, 21 April 2009, *Enerji Yapi-Yol Sen v. Turkey* (application no. 68959/01), which applies this method to protecting the right to strike.

visibility of human rights, this method enables the ECHR to make sure that fundamental social rights are respected. At the same time, however, the European Court of Justice, as we have seen, endeavours to empty them of all content.[13] The conflict between these supra-national jurisdictions is clear for all to see, and the best solution would doubtless be for the Council of Europe to set the ECHR on a firm legal footing and enable it to pursue its new role as guardian of fundamental social rights. As soon as a specific jurisdiction is created to ensure that the goal of social justice is respected, as encoded in a number of international legal instruments from the Declaration of Philadelphia onwards, a 'social Europe' will cease to be a hollow promise. It is a goal which generates duties as much as rights, and such a jurisdiction could, for example, in its application of the principle of solidarity, sanction practices – currently encouraged by the European Court of Justice – of social or fiscal dumping by member states, or of law shopping by companies that seek to dodge the tax or welfare contributions to which their activities give rise. These practices cannot be defined simply as unfair competition or tax evasion. They constitute more fundamental infringements, namely violations of human rights as enshrined for the economic and social fields in the Universal Declaration of 1948, and they should be characterised and cracked down on as such.

A DIVERSITY OF REPRESENTATIONAL SYSTEMS: THE PRACTICE OF MEASURE

Social justice is a principle of action. As such, its successful implementation relies on an accurate representation of the facts, and it cannot be reduced to the application of a system of predefined rules. Indeed, one of the particularities of social law – which did not escape the

---

13 See above, chap. 3.

first jurists to take the field seriously, before the Second World War – was that it called for *discovery* as much as *application* of a rule. An equitable distribution of rights and duties for everyone can emerge only by setting divergent interests alongside one another, and arriving at a provisional compromise, which can always be revised. This inductive method is familiar to common law traditions, but it has always been perceived as alien in the codifying traditions of Romano-canonic law. In common law, the judge decides on the rule in the light of his experience of a diversity of cases, an experience which he represents and which lends legitimacy to his pronouncement of the law. In the continental tradition, by contrast, the judge is in theory only the 'mouth that pronounces the words of the law', in the famous words of Montesquieu. The judge judges, for example, 'in the name of the French people', and so has the role of the people's legal representative, but in fact does nothing other, in exercising his 'own' will, than apply what has already been expressed in the laws passed by a parliament, where the people have their sole space of democratic representation.

The systems of representation needed to further social justice are not easy to situate in relation to these earlier forms. The failure of attempts to introduce compulsory arbitration to settle industrial disputes has shown that such disputes cannot be resolved by appeal to precedent. The social democratic process borrows from parliamentary representation the eminently democratic idea that, in order to be just, a legal norm must proceed from a representation of all those to whom it is to be applied. But, unlike parliamentary representation, it does not have an individualist and quantitative basis (one man, one vote), but a collective and qualitative one (one interest group, one vote). In this respect it adopts a much older form of representation, one which sought to give a faithful representation of the variety of social conditions (similar to the Estates General under the *ancien régime*), rather than grounding a fiction of unanimity in a numerical majority. Social democracy aims at what Pierre Rosanvallon calls a 'legitimacy of reflexivity',[14] which does not seek to achieve majority agreement, but rather to create consensus as to what course of action is the most just (or least unjust) at a specific time and under specific circumstances. Since it accepts qualitative differences between interest groups, which have a different experience of the same facts, it does not *presuppose* equality between these groups but *constructs* it, by making sure that there is a balance of power between them. This balance is achieved, for example, by recognising the right to strike and, more recently in France, the majority principle for trade union representation in collective bargaining. In a social democracy, rights to worker representation, to strike action and to collective bargaining are some of the mechanisms by which power relations can be channelled into legal form.

Despite their differences, parliamentary and social democracy have two features in common: they aspire to take into account the full diversity of human experience, and they use collective deliberation as a way of arriving at decisions which can be deemed just.[15] The forms of representation characterising governance, by contrast, aim at quantifying facts rather than reflecting experience, at counting rather than conferring. It is principally through accounting, statistics and indicators that governance achieves its quantified representation of the world. Each of these forms is legitimate and has its own

14   P. Rosanvallon, *La légitimité démocratique: Impartialité, réflexivité, proximité*, Paris: Seuil, 2008.
15   This fruitful concept of *assemblée de parole* ('discussion forum') was introduced by Marcel Détienne. See his *Comparing the Incomparable*, trans. Janet Lloyd, Palo Alto: Stanford University Press, 2008; and a volume that Détienne edited, *Qui veut prendre la parole?*, Paris: Seuil, 2003.

sphere of validity. Accounting aims to 'give a true and fair view' of the financial situation and financial results of a company.[16] Statistics, as the name indicates, aims to provide the state with a scientific representation of society.[17] As for indicators, which really came into their own with the birth of the welfare state,[18] they are signs of the social body's 'physiology', as well as sign-posts for government policy relating to it. The success of these quantified forms of representation of society reflects a desire to manage human affairs in a scientific manner. This is at once their strength and their danger. Their strength, because the objectified representation of the world to which indicators aspire can enable agreement on what would be a fair rule to follow; their danger, because this can lead to the dog-matic illusion that this representation is really scientific truth. Unlike the science of weights and measures, which seeks to represent a reality independent of and pre-existing the measurer, accounting and statistical instruments invent the very categories they account for, by recourse to conventions of equivalence through which qualitatively different situations are correlated to the same quantitative measure.[19] This process invites a fetishistic fixation on the sign and the pursuit of the mirage of quantification in which the thing itself disap-pears behind its quantified representation, and policy goals come to be focused on improving statistical or

16 On this legal definition, see Y. Lemarchand, 'Le miroir du marchand', in *Tisser le lien social*, ed. Alain Supiot, Paris: Éd. de la MSH, 2004, 213.

17 'Statistics' comes from the German *Statistik*, which in turn derives from *Staat*, 'state'.

18 See A. Desrosières, 'Refléter ou instituer. L'invention des indicateurs statistiques', 1997; repr. in *Pour une sociologie historique de la quantification*, Paris: Presses de l'École des Mines, 2008, 187ff.

19 On employment statistics, see the seminal work by R. Salais, N. Baverez and B. Reynaud, *L'invention du chômage*, Paris: PUF, 1986.

accounting scores, while reality itself recedes.[20] In the recent collapse of the financial markets and, more generally, in the failures of today's dominant management method for both companies and nations – namely, governance by numbers – it is precisely this fetishism which has come to light.

In this context, it will take more than singing the praises of social dialogue, or the three-way negotiations introduced by the ILO, to reinstate the imperative of social democracy. We need to make sure that the concrete effects of globalisation are permanently measured up against the objective of social justice. This presupposes taking social democracy out of its present ghetto and bringing it up to date in the light of the diversification of types of work in the modern world. The major obstacle to this is not, despite what discussions on the 'articulation of law and contract' might lead one to believe, the nature of the link between social and political democracy. Not that this is not a real issue, but the terms of the debate have already been established, and a certain number of institutional mechanisms are already in place to secure this 'articulation' (which is actually more of a hybridisation). The really pressing issue is, rather, how to articulate these two forms of deliberative representation on the one hand with, on the other, the quantified representations of the state of the world which the ideology of governance fetishises and which it refuses to submit to any deliberative process. Even 'human development indicators', which are conceived and implemented with the best of intentions,[21] are no exception, in that they project onto the whole globe a normativity which is oblivious

---

20 See above, chap. 3. See also R. Salais, 'Usages et mésusages de l'argument statistique: le pilotage des politiques publiques par la performance'.
21 See J. Gadrey and F. Jany-Catrice, *Les nouveaux indicateurs de richesse*, Paris: La Découverte, 2007.

to local contexts. Prohibiting 'child labour' in general and abstract terms, and making school attendance rates into a 'human development indicator' can mean tearing children away from traditional modes of transmission of knowledge and cramming them by the hundreds into vast prefabs with a teacher who is overwhelmed by the sheer numbers. The country's score will improve in the eyes of international organisations, but the real state of education will come out of it considerably worse.[22]

Two examples will give an idea of how the democratic process could harness the techniques of quantification in the interests of social justice. The first concerns international accounting standardisation. This technique has degenerated into a method for benchmarking the short-term financial performance of companies. It no longer plays the role of reminding economic decision-makers of their responsibilities, but simply treats human activity as a liability on the balance sheet.[23] This has the further undesired effect of giving a distorted image of the value of the company and enlisting it in a scramble for 'value creation' divorced from the real economy. The measures introduced in France after the Second World War to ensure that companies adopted open-book policies for employee representatives were useful, but they address the situation only after the accounting standards themselves have been defined. Despite the fact that the latter express normative choices which are determinant on the just redistribution of wealth, they escape any democratic deliberative process. No 'accounting truth' can dispense with discussions involving both

22   For Mali, see O. Sidibé, 'Les indicateurs de performance améliorent-ils l'efficacité de l'aide au développement?', *Journal de l'Institut d'études avancées de Nantes*, online at iea-nantes.fr.
23   Samuel Jubé argues this point most convincingly in *Droit social et normalisation comptable*, Paris: LGDJ lextenso, 2011.

parliamentary and trade union representation.[24] The second example concerns international norms and standards of work. The ILO's standards resemble a storehouse of rules where countries (and on occasion multinationals feeling low on 'social responsibility') can come and shop for whatever rules they wish to apply. This approach ignores the innovative dimension of the Declaration of Philadelphia, which defines social justice in terms of objectives, of policy guidelines, and not simply in terms of rules to be applied. A new type of standard is needed. It would require countries to adhere to a certain number of core principles pertaining to 'decent work'; and it would commit them contractually to determining, with the help of international financial institutions and in consultation with worker organisations, how these standards will be implemented at local or national level.[25] Such consultation should include defining the indicators appropriate for particular environments and best able to show how the implementation of the guidelines is progressing. This combination of a universal objective of social justice with the representation of local conditions of work should prevent 'salaried employment' and 'human development' from being projected as paradigms onto the whole planet.

24 See B. Colasse, *Les fondements de la comptabilité*, Paris: La Découverte, 2007, 77ff.
25 See A. Supiot 'Social Protection and Decent Work: New Prospects for International Labour Standards', in *Comparative Labor Law and Policy Journal*, 27:2, 2006.

7

THE CAPACITY TO ACT

In the cybernetic world of regulation and governance, human beings do not *act*. They *re*act to the signals received from the information systems to which they are connected. And they do not talk to each other, they communicate, by means of these systems. This gradual process of substituting reaction for action and communication for conversation does not only affect lower-skilled workers, of whom it is expected that they will be 'an adaptable workforce . . . responsive to economic change' (Treaty on the Functioning of the EU, art. 145), but also those at the top of the hierarchy. Company directors react to the signals produced by the financial markets, just as political leaders react to opinion polls. And the higher the position in the hierarchy, the greater the requirement to 'communicate', rather than converse.

In the Declaration of Philadelphia, economic prosperity presupposes free individuals and not flexibly reactive ones, which is why, once again, we must return to its ethos in order to reinstate the capacity to act. If we accept, in its words, that 'freedom of expression and of association are essential to sustained progress' (art. Ib) and that 'all human beings . . . have the right to pursue both their material well-being and their spiritual development in conditions of *freedom* and dignity, of *economic security* and equal opportunity' (art. IIa, my emphases), then we must also accept that the goal to be pursued by countries and international organisations is not to make workers 'employable', but to enable them to obtain 'the satisfaction of giving the fullest measure of their skill and attainments and make their greatest contribution to the common well-being' (art. IIIb). The emphasis placed on freedom in one's work was something radically new in 1944, and it broke with the pact on which industrial society had been based, namely that the worker's renunciation of his or her freedom in the workplace was a technical, not a political, constraint, and hence that social justice concerned the distribution, not the creation, of wealth. It took the exceptional lucidity of Simone Weil, and her experience of industrial labour,[1] for Taylorism to be criticised at all in the pre-war period, while Lenin was calling it 'a huge step forward in scientific progress'.[2] As Bruno Trentin has shown convincingly in his classic work *La città del lavoro*,[3] trade unions and left-leaning political parties in socialist and capitalist countries alike were convinced very early on that workers must accept a scientific organisation of labour, and that this was a matter of efficiency, not of justice. After the crisis of 1929, big business, for its part, held that increased wages and economic security for employees were not only legitimate goals, but additionally brought efficiency gains in terms of productivity and sales opportunities.

This founding pact came apart some thirty years

1 See particularly S. Weil, 'Reflections Concerning the Causes of Liberty and Social Oppression', in *Oppression and Liberty*, New York and London: Routledge, 2001, 36–117; and 'La rationalisation' (1937) in *La condition ouvrière*, Paris: Gallimard, 1951, 289–90.

2 Quoted by J. Querzola, 'Le chef d'orchestre à la main de fer. Léninisme et taylorisme', in *Le soldat du travail. Recherches* 32/33, Sept. 1978, 58.

3 B. Trentin, *La città del lavoro. Sinistra e crisi del fordismo*, Milan: Feltrinelli, 1997.

ago, partly due to the free circulation of capital and the competition introduced between Northern and Southern workforces, and partly because of techno-logical progress and the impact it had on work and its organisation. Left-leaning trade unions and the politi-cal left proved incapable of thinking through this new situation, and they hesitated between clinging to inherited advantages and 'accompanying' workers forced into casual and poorly-paid jobs.[4] But 'reform', as it is understood in the history of the labour move-ment, has never meant adapting to the world's injustices, but rather mobilising the theoretical and practical means to combat these. In this light, we need to think through the crisis in the Fordist industrial model to see how it could give rise to improved condi-tions for the greatest number rather than to the destruction of worker-protection schemes and the return of unbridled exploitation of the weak. This destruction naturally goes by the name of 'individual freedoms': freedom to be paid less than the contractu-ally agreed rate, freedom to work fifteen hours a day and never retire, freedom to work Sundays rather than spend it with one's children, freedom never to go to court to uphold one's rights, freedom to prostitute oneself, and so forth. The same perversion of lan-guage is at work in the expression 'labour value' (used to justify reduced taxation on capital rather than increased wage levels) or 'value creation' (which no longer refers to labour but to the income generated from the financial pillage of companies, when it is not

---

4 'Accompanying change' has become one of the buzz words of European social policy. See the communication from the Commission, *Restructuring and Employment – Anticipating and Accompanying Restructuring in Order to Develop Employment: The Role of the European Union* (COM/2005/0120 final), which gave rise to the establishment of a 'European Globalisation Adjustment Fund', and even to a new individual right (see F. Petit, 'Le droit à l'accompagnement', *Droit Social*, 2008, 413–23).

from 'creative accounting'). As Orwell realised, this denaturing of language is typical of the thought police,[5] and reclaiming the proper sense of words is a necessary first step towards having a purchase over one's future. Contrary to what the slogan 'There is no alternative', dear to the followers of the neo-liberal revolution, would have us believe, the disintegration of the Fordist model faces us precisely with a choice. The problem is that this choice has not yet managed to find political expression.

As early as the 1930s, Simone Weil's experience as a factory worker led her to conclude that 'the worker's complete subordination to the undertaking and to those who run it is founded on the factory organization and not on the system of property'.[6] It was an analysis which at the time could only fall on deaf ears, since this industrial structure was considered integral to a scientific organisation of labour, in capitalist and communist countries alike. The Fordist pact, which consisted in making workers accept this arrangement in exchange for a certain degree of material security, undermined any contestation of a conception of work where 'things play the role of human beings and human beings play the role of things'.[7] The collapse of the Fordist pact provides us with an opportunity to imagine a new labour pact based not on subordinating and programming workers but on valuing their freedom and their responsibility. This was the orientation recommended some ten years ago in the report

5 See 'Appendix: The Principles of Newspeak', in his *1984*, New York and London: Penguin Signet, 1981, 299–312. 'The purpose of Newspeak', writes Orwell, 'was not only to provide a medium of expression for the world-view and mental habits proper to the devotees of IngSoc, but to make all other modes of thought impossible.'

6 S. Weil, 'Reflections Concerning the Causes of Liberty and Social Oppression', in *Oppression and Liberty*, 40.

7 S. Weil, 'Expérience de la vie d'usine' (1941), in *La condition ouvrière*, Paris: Gallimard, 1951, 337.

commissioned by the European Commission on the transformations of work and the future of labour law in Europe, *Beyond Employment*.[8] It laid the foundations for a legal framework for membership of the workforce which would allow real and lifelong freedom of choice, movement from one employment situation to another, and the harmonisation of private and working life. When the employment contract no longer provides long-term economic security for workers, another status must be invented which provides equivalent security. Examining work 'beyond employment' was not to suggest that employment would disappear (just as work 'beyond the borders of France' does not imply the disappearance of France), and indeed employment remains an essential dimension of occupational status. Rather, it means that employment no longer provides – if it ever did – a normative framework capable of ensuring that all people, across the world, can have access to decent work.

These proposals certainly helped refresh trade union thinking, and their goals were reformulated in terms of 'social security for working life' or 'securing career paths' (the French trade union confederations CGT and CFDT, respectively). But European institutions did not take up the simple idea on which they were based: that wealth is a human creation and any normative system which puts things above human beings will not stand the test of time. For, logically, the definition of the socio-political matrix of human beings must precede that of their relations to things, without which their actions make no sense.[9] The notions of 'status as

8 A. Supiot (ed.), *Beyond Employment: Changes in Work and the Future of Labour Law in Europe*, Oxford: Oxford University Press, 2005.

9 This is the order in Gaius's *Institutes*: 'Omne autem jus quo utimur vel at personas pertinet, vel at res, vel ad actiones. Sed prius videamus de personis' ('The whole of the law by which we are governed relates either to persons, or to things, or to actions; and let us first examine the

member of the workforce' or of 'social drawing
rights' are based on this fundamental principle, and
they could hardly be further removed from our contemporary belief that, rather than adapting the
economy to the needs of human beings, we should be
making human beings adapt to the demands of the
market, and especially to the financial markets, which
are supposed to usher in a reign of harmony by treating all financial activity as a calculable quantity.
Whereas regulating these markets should have been a
top priority, the European Commission – in this no
different from the other major international organisations for economic affairs – had only one obsession
and one slogan, to 'reform the labour markets' in
order to force people to accept 'the permanent reshap-
ing of the fabric of production'[10] and so maximise
'value creation' for those playing the economy as
though it were some kind of gambling den. This is
why, in its recent publications and, for example, in
'Modernising Labour Law' (its Green Book of 2006),
the Commission serves up once again, with the pre-
dictability of a well-trained parrot, its plate of
platitudes concerning the 'rigidity' of employment-
protection schemes – a point of view shared, moreover,
by the 'elites' of all member states, whatever their
political colour.

The spirit of Philadelphia exhorts us, on the contrary, to enable workers to give 'the full measure of
their skill and attainments and make their greatest contribution to the common well-being'. In other words,
workers must have the concrete means to exercise their
freedom of action. Acting freely is not obeying or

law of persons'). See Gaius. *Institutes of Roman Law,* tr. Edward Poste,
Oxford: Clarendon Press, 1904, I, §8.

10   See the European Commission, *Restructuring and Employment –
Anticipating and Accompanying Restructuring in Order to Develop
Employment: The Role of the European Union* (COM/2005/0120 final).

reacting; and without economic security no one can act freely, since any action supposes the capacity to act. It should be the policy of countries and international organisations to support workers' capacities and enable them to express their talents.

A person's capacity, in the legal sense, is his or her ability to enter into contract. In other words, capacity has the particularity of partaking at once of civil status and of contract law. It is what prevents the contract from being simply a mechanical instrument, independent of the identity and aptitudes of the contracting parties, and as such is considered by some to be vital to a viable market economy on a global scale. The concept of capacity comes from Roman law and has the advantage of forming part of the legal heritage of Europe, common to continental and common law countries alike, unlike the notions of 'capability'[11] or 'professional status', which are specific to one or other of the two legal cultures. It could therefore function as a common normative reference for the European Union and guide our attempts to rethink social citizenship at a time when the welfare systems and solidarities inherited from the industrial era are coming apart. The notion of capacity would have to be extended beyond its present scope, that is, beyond the conditions of age and soundness of mind to which a contractual agreement is already subject. It could then, in particular, help us rethink the role of public services on a European scale, since their quality and accessibility have a significant impact on people's ability to act.

As comparative analysis has shown, the concept of a person's capacity is already gaining ground in a good

---

11 For this notion, see A. Sen, *Commodities and Capabilities*, Oxford: Oxford University Press, 1999; R. Salais and R. Villeneuve (eds.), *Europe and the Politics of Capabilities*, Cambridge: Cambridge University Press, 2005.

number of European countries,[12] particularly, in the last few years, the notion of 'professional capacity'. Until recently, the expression was confined, more or less, to the legal conditions for practising a particular profession. More generally, 'professional capacity' is one of the criteria determining which jobs an unemployed person can occupy. But in labour law the notion is much more innovative: it designates not only a condition for exercising a particular activity, but also the object of a contractual obligation. French law has recently established an employer's obligation to ensure that his or her employees maintain their capacity to continue in employment, and the *Cour de cassation*, the highest court in the French judiciary, has upheld the decision.[13]

The notion of capacity could also help us rethink the forms of collective action available to employees. Labour law is unique and uniquely modern in recognising that the capacity of individuals is anchored in that of the groups to which they belong, and that society is not and cannot be the cloud of contracting particles to which market fundamentalists wish to reduce it. The ILO's Declaration of 1998, which contains four fundamental principles and rights, formulates the first of these as 'Freedom of association and the effective recognition of the right to collective bargaining'. This highlights two aspects of 'collective capacity': on the one hand the capacity of individuals to organise freely and act collectively to defend their economic and work interests (freedom of association and right to strike); and on the other hand the capacity of

---

12   See S. Deakin and A. Supiot (eds.), *Capacitas: Contract Law and the Institutional Preconditions of a Market Economy*, Oxford: Hart, 2009.

13   See article L. 6321-1 of the French Labour Code (law of 4 May 2004), and the ruling *Union des opticiens* by the *Cour de cassation*, 23 Oct. 2007 (no. 06-40950).

organisations to draw up collective agreements (rights to collective bargaining).

In order for power relations to be channelled into legal form, labour law must rest on three supports: collective organisation, collective action and collective bargaining. If one of these is missing, the legal structure will be off balance, and the law will no longer metabolise the potential sources of violence in society. This is what we see happening today, since freedom to associate and to strike are confined within national legal frameworks, while free enterprise is not. This situation not only creates an imbalance between trade unions and large companies, but it effectively cripples the right to strike. First, because the increasing numbers of casual workers are not able to strike. Second, because strike action only makes sense in the context of a confrontation between a body of employees and a clearly identifiable employer from whom they take their orders. This type of one-on-one relation is often lacking today. The group cohesion of the workforce is often fragmented by outsourcing, subcontracting and temporary contracts, and those who really take the decisions may not be the employer, and may evade their responsibilities by hiding behind the fronts of the different companies economically dependent on them. In such circumstances, strike action tends to become the weapon of the strong, while the weak have no access to it. The pilots of a national airline can go on strike, whereas the baggage handlers, who are contracted in, cannot. Since the tensions produced by the exploitation of labour can no longer find expression in the field of collective action, they find expression in particularist claims. The way the trade union movement has degenerated into corporatist interests, on the one hand, and the withdrawal into religious, ethnic or sexual identity politics on the other are two sides of the same coin. What we need in this context is to reform rights to collective action, so that weaker members of the workforce can regain the capacity to influence their future collectively. Looking further ahead, forms of collective action involving third parties, for example consumers or investors, should be explored, since these can constitute a useful weapon in the face of the contemporary transformations of free enterprise. A counter-balance could thus be found to the free circulation of goods and capital through a broader range of forms of international collective action.

The concept of capacity would therefore help reverse, if not completely halt, the tendency today to invert (economic) means and (human) ends. This inversion is particularly clear in the language cultivated by European institutions and permeated by what Bruno Romano calls 'functional fundamentalism'.[14] 'Human beings', 'professional capacities' and 'freedoms' have all disappeared, in favour of 'human capital',[15] 'employability' and 'flexibility'. In these terminological shifts, modes of thought derived from physics and biology replace legal categories, and show how people are treated like things. The idea of human capital, which was popularised by Stalin[16] before being adopted by contemporary economic theory,[17] was the Communist equivalent of the Nazi notion of 'human material'. It reflects a scientistic vision of the world in

14 B. Romano, *Fondalismo funzionale e nichilismo giuridico. Postumanesimo 'noia' globalizzatione*, Turin: Giappichelli, 2000.

15 See the European Council's decision concerning the guidelines for member states' employment policy (2006/544/CE, *Journal Officiel* L 215 of 5.8.2006, 26–7), which make 'increasing investment in human capital' a priority.

16 See J.V. Stalin, *Works*, vol. 14: *1934–1940*, London: Red Star Press, 1978.

17 G. Becker, *Human Capital: A Theoretical and Empirical Analysis, with Special Reference to Education*, Chicago: University of Chicago Press, 1964.

which human beings are no more than an economic resource.[18] Likewise for the notion of 'employability', which, in the etymological sense, means forcing people to bow to the needs of the markets,[19] rather than taking as a starting-point their intelligence and creativity, that is, their professional capacities. As for the notion of flexibility, it conflates workers and materials, whereas arguing in terms of freedom of action would oblige one to reconcile freedom of enterprise and freedom of work, and would engage with what – not only in the circulation of goods and capital, but also in the minds and work of human beings – is always new and surprising.

The pessimistic idea that legal categories will inevitably be dissolved into managerial and cybernetic discourses is doubtless unfounded, despite its seductive power. It is a utopia which the West has pursued for the last two centuries, that of replacing the government of men by the administration of things. The fact that it holds particular fascination for today's world does not mean that it is not utopian, and therefore destined, like all utopias, to run up against the reality principle one day or another. There seemed to be a consensus, for instance, that in an economy, security was only important for things (security for financial, business and legal operations), whereas

---

18 Strictly speaking, 'human capital' designates the assets held by a slave-owner. See C.S. McWatters and Y. Lemarchand, 'Comptabilité et traite négrière', in J.G. Degos and S. Trébucq (eds.), *L'entreprise, le chiffre et le droit*, Bordeaux: Université Montesquieu, 2005, 209–36.

19 The definition of 'employability' given by the European Commission is as follows: 'A person is employable when he or she has the marketable skills, competence or features which are regarded by labour market demand as necessary conditions for hiring.' Cit. Ph. Pochet and M. Paternotre, *'Employabilité' dans le contexte des lignes directrices de l'Union européenne sur l'emploi*, Observatoire Social Européen, 1998.

economic security for people, which was one of the
goals set for trade and finance policy in the Declaration
of Philadelphia, was to disappear and be replaced by
a positive principle of insecurity designed to make
people flexible and to adapt them to the needs of the
market. But this principle comes up against the realities of human existence, and the long time of the
succession of generations, which require securities
different from those of the market. Even the lowliest
of jobs draws on the long time of education and
training, and the greater the real economic security
and work skills of workers, the more 'efficient' they
will be. This is why the hybrid term 'flexicurity'
emerged in EU terminology.[20] We should of course
welcome the EU's discovery of basic human needs,
but attempting to stick together different concepts
within the same word produces more of a fantastical
chimera than an operative concept. Simone Weil
noted in 1936 that 'Were we to have to endure both
the subjection of the slave and the risks of the free
man, it would be too much.'[21] This is precisely the
crisis we will face if those who champion workers'
initiative and autonomy at the same time treat workers like objects at the disposal of the market. One has
only to compare, term for term, the concepts contained respectively in the notions of 'flexicurity' and
'social and economic rights' (flexibility / freedom,
employability / capacity, human capital / membership of the workforce) to grasp how they differ. In
the first case, the starting point is the supposed infallibility of the market, and the aim is to provide a
human 'resource' adapted to the immediate needs of

20   European Commission, *Towards Common Principles of Flexicurity:
More and Better Jobs Through Flexibility and Security*, Communication
of 27 June 2007 (COM/2007/359 final).
21   S. Weil, 'Lettre à un ingénieur', *La Condition ouvrière*, Paris:
Gallimard, 1951, 187.

companies; in the second, the starting point is human creativity, and the aim is to establish a legal system and an economy through which it may best find expression.

8

THE ONUS OF RESPONSIBILITY

A person is deemed 'responsible' when he or she is obliged to answer for his acts before another. The root of this notion is the solemn promise of Roman law, in which the *spondeo* of a first party is echoed by the *respondeo* of a second. This exchange of promises, which was originally accompanied by a libation to the gods, endows the promises with binding force.[1] The acts for which one is responsible may be legal or physical in nature, or even consist of abstaining from action, but responsibility is present if, and only if, one can impute these acts to a specific subject who is answerable for them before a third party. Responsibility therefore implies a three-way relationship between three parties: the person who is responsible and therefore to whom the act can be imputed as its cause;[2] the plaintiff,

---

1 On the religious origin of the concept, see E. Benveniste, *Indo-European Language and Society*, trans. Elizabeth Palmer, Coral Gables, Fl.: University of Miami Press, 1967; M. Villey, 'Esquisse historique du mot responsable', *Archives de philosophie du droit*, vol. 22: *La responsabilité*, Sirey, 1977, 46ff.

2 On the difference between imputation, which is specific to legal technique, and scientific causality, see H. Kelsen, *Pure Theory of Law*, trans. Max Knight, Berkeley: University of California Press, 1967; also, by the same author, *General Theory of Norms*, trans. Michael Hartney, Oxford: Oxford University Press, 1990.

whose interests are affected by the act; and a third (judge or arbiter) before whom the person responsible may be held accountable for his acts. As such, responsibility or liability does not mean only the obligation to make reparation for the harmful consequences of one's acts but also the obligation to prevent them and to agree to be held accountable for them if they arise. In contemporary tort law, the duty of foresight and of assuming responsibility have taken on ever greater importance as the risks attendant upon scientific and technological progress have increased.

Enterprise, in its primary sense, is what mobilises technological resources more than any other activity, and therefore represents a major risk factor. The issue of industrial injury and the risks involved in new business developments led all industrialised countries to develop civil liability legislation at the turn of the twentieth century, and to introduce the idea of a strict liability, which was not founded on an actual offence by the person responsible, but on the risk which the person's activity represented for others. Further developments depended on the country. In French law, for instance, this idea of strict liability led to more extensive obligations to be insured, whereas other countries tended to restrict this method to hazardous activities or products. American law developed the possibility of class actions, with juries quick to pass stiff sentences on big business,[3] whereas French law generally remained committed to an individualistic conception of legal action (with the exception of labour law). Beyond these differences, however, companies are nowadays obliged, wherever they may be, to take into consideration interests other than their own in how they run their affairs. Milton Friedman could

---

3   See J.G. Fleming, *The American Tort Process*, Oxford: Clarendon Press, 1988; M. Fabre-Magnan, *Droit des obligations*, vol. 2: *Responsabilité civile et quasi-contrats*, Paris: PUF, 2007, no. 87, 207ff.

state, a few years before being awarded the economics prize 'in memory of Alfred Nobel', that 'the only social responsibility of business is to increase its profits',[4] but only a national legal and political framework which obliges companies to assume the consequences of their actions on men and nature can sustain such a mono-functional vision of business enterprise.

Since no such framework exists at the international level, the notion of 'corporate social responsibility' (CSR) is meant to make up for it. Multinationals present themselves as states in miniature, with concerns other than making money for their shareholders.[5] But where there is no clearly identifiable entity to which responsibility can be assigned, where no organisation exists which may call companies to account, and without a third party to hear the case, this 'responsibility' is clearly bogus. CSR is more the symptom of a crisis affecting an economistic ideology than a convincing cure for the aberrations engendered by globalisation. Now that the abolition of trade barriers has enabled companies to throw off the constraints of national legislation and operate in a legal no-man's land, the economy's unacknowledged dogmatic foundations have re-emerged and instigated a quest for debtors, creditors and arbiters, without which no one is responsible for anything.

In the codes of good practice concerning the social responsibility of business enterprises, the notion of 'enterprise' is most often taken for granted. The European Commission's communication on the subject,[6] for

---

4   M. Friedman, 'The Social Responsibility of Business Is to Increase Its Profits', *The New York Times Magazine*, 13 Sept. 1970, 32–3, 122–4.

5   From an extensive bibliography on this subject, see T. Berns, et al., *Responsabilités des entreprises et corégulation*, Brussels: Bruylant, 2007.

6   Communication from the European Commission of 2 July 2002: *Corporate Social Responsibility: A Business Contribution to Sustainable Development* (COM/2002/347), § 3.

instance, does not give a definition. It simply notes that 'the CSR concept was developed mainly by and for large multinational enterprises' and, in its inimitable style, announces that it will 'foster CSR among SMEs'.[7] Likewise, the codes of good practice developed by major international organisations such as the OECD *Guidelines* or the ILO's *Tripartite Declaration* seem uncomfortable with the issue, a fact they attempt to conceal behind the commanding tone they adopt: for the OECD, 'A precise definition of multinational enterprises is not required',[8] and the ILO's Declaration 'does not require a precise legal definition of multinational enterprises'.[9] However, each then goes on to propose a definition – and they are quite similar – while also stating, in the case of the ILO, that the definition is no definition at all . . .[10]

We can well understand the difficulty experienced by these international organisations in their attempts to give an exact description of the 'entities' for which their codes of good corporate practice are designed. 'Enterprise' is, first, an activity grounded in the freedom of enterprise, which as such can never quite be institutionalised. The legal situation is straightforward when the entrepreneur is present in person as a tradesman. When he or she establishes a company that is the same as the business enterprise and gives the latter legal form, the situation is still simple to grasp. Things get a bit more complicated when that company creates subsidiaries or comes under the financial management of another, and thus becomes part of a constantly

7 COM/2002/347, cit. above, § 4.5.

8 OECD *Guidelines for Multinational Enterprises*, 1976 (rev. 2000), § 1.3.

9 ILO *Tripartite Declaration of Principles concerning Multinational Enterprises and Social Policy*, 1977 (rev. 2000), § 6.

10 The *Tripartite Declaration* states that 'this paragraph is designed to facilitate the understanding of the Declaration and not to provide such a definition'.

changing and ill-defined group of companies. And the situation becomes positively opaque when the company becomes part of a network of companies which are mutually independent in terms of capital holdings but linked through contractual bonds of dependence, for example in the case of subcontracting or patent licensing. This kind of reticular organisation dissolves the management pole of labour relations, which is sometimes difficult or even impossible to identify. The notion of an enterprise is therefore less and less true to its original sense of 'firm' (from the Latin *firmus*, 'solid', which first meant 'signature' in English and gradually, by extension, the name under which a company operates). The company's freedom of legal organisation has become a way for the entrepreneur to disappear behind a plethora of legal personalities which disguise rather than identify him on the scene of exchange, and enable him to shirk the responsibilities incurred by his economic activity.

One of the major legal problems arising from the free international circulation of goods and capital is precisely that of identifying who the real economic operators are. We can learn a lot from comparing environmental and social legislation, which is something the idea of CSR encourages us to do. When an ecological catastrophe occurs, such as the *Erika* or *Prestige* oil spills, it takes months to identify the real decision-makers, if indeed one ever manages to do so. In the case of the *Prestige*, for instance, the inquiry came up against Panamanian law, which effectively guarantees their anonymity.[11] The tanker might as well have flown a black pirate's flag – which, as we know, has never boded well for the honest merchant. The employer's immunity is not a problem solely in maritime

---

11 See the excellent article by M. Roche, 'Où sont passés les responsables du *Prestige*?', *Le Monde*, 21 Nov. 2003, which unpicks in detail the mechanisms of concealment employed.

matters, but more generally in all companies with a complex structure in which the financial stakeholders attempt, as Milton Friedman would have it, to maximise profits and evade responsibilities. Criminal business law was the first to describe this problem of identifying the real economic operators,[12] but it has also become a major issue in consumer law, in the wake of public health crises like asbestos or mad cow disease, and more recently in financial law, with the collapse of the banking sector and the reappearance of states as the ultimate guarantors of the colossal debts the banks had accumulated. Labour law has also shown that it is possible to get behind the legal foils of business law to identify the real company director(s) when public imperatives such as health and security, the prevention of illegal employment, and collective employee representation are at stake. But however ingenious these techniques may be, they still only have a purchase within national frontiers, which companies precisely can ignore, given the free circulation of goods and capital.

This touches on the Achilles' heel of our legal systems, namely the notion of a legal subject and the need to be able to impute the responsibility for an act, or a prejudicial failure to act, to a specific person. In view of this, and if the idea of corporate social responsibility is to have any credibility, we can envisage, broadly, two solutions.

The first is solidarity in liability between what are legally different parts of a same business enterprise. One can counter Milton Friedman's principle that 'the only social responsibility of business is to increase its profits', with the adage from Roman law, *Ubi emolumentum, ibi onus* (Whoever experiences the benefit bears the burden, and is therefore liable). It implies that all those benefiting from an economic

---

12   See P. Lascoumes, *Les affaires ou l'art de l'ombre. Les délinquances économiques et financières et leur contrôle*, Paris: Le Centurion, 1986.

activity must be considered as operators, whatever the legal constructions used by the business. This interpretation was used in the United States to great effect in the field of maritime pollution: ever since the *Exxon Valdes* oil spill, American law provides for prosecution of all those who take part in a transport operation, however minor their role.[13] This is a move in which the primary sense of 'solidarity', as inherited from Roman law, is reasserted, whereas it had long been eclipsed by techniques borrowed from insurance: 'There is joint and several liability (*solidarité*) on the part of debtors where they are bound for a same thing, so that each one may be compelled for the whole, and payment made by one alone discharges the others towards the creditor' (French Civil Code, art. 1200). CSR cannot function without this sort of solidarity between the different parts of a supply chain or a transnational network. It is an idea that is already applied in domestic labour law,[14] and one can make a convincing case for international private law also being interpreted in the light of the principle of social justice, since it serves to determine the jurisdiction of courts and the applicability of a law to a dispute.[15] In which case, one could identify the entities 'able to exercise a significant influence over the activities of others' (as the OECD *Guidelines* puts it), and make them liable for any behaviour in contravention of the *Guidelines* on the part of entities belonging to the same supply chain or network

---

13 The American Oil Pollution Act of 1990 provides that responsibility for pollution caused by a vessel rests with 'any person owning, operating, or demise chartering the vessel'.

14 For example, concerning temporary employment, subcontracting and undeclared work, and in matters of health and security. See E. Peskine, *Réseaux d'entreprises et droit du travail*, Paris: LGDJ, 2008.

15 See U. Baxi, 'Mass Torts, Multinational Enterprise Liability and Private International Law', *Recueil des cours de l'Académie de droit international de La Haye* 276, 1999, 301–427.

established in a 'host country'. This interpretation would encourage good practice in subcontracting (and discourage bad practice), as confirmed by the American Oil Pollution Act, whose introduction has had the effect of making large petroleum companies more attentive to safety issues in the choice of their carriers. And even in the absence of special legislation of this sort, Tort law can provide ample grounds for making multinationals assume their liability for the violation of fundamental workers' rights in the countries to which these companies relocate their activities. Such a method, based on creating bonds of solidarity between trade unions in the North and workers in the South, has been used successfully in the US and is a model which could usefully be imported into Europe.[16]

The second solution involves making products traceable so that the person responsible for first putting them into circulation on a market can be held to account. This was the approach adopted in Community law regarding liability for defective products.[17] The new swathe of civil liability legislation developed is characterised by the fact that 'The producer shall be liable for damage caused by a defect in his product' (art. 1 of the Directive; and article 1386-1 of the French Civil Code adds: 'whether he was bound by a contract with the injured person or not'). This makes it possible to go straight to the person who first put a product into circulation – or the importer of the product who 'shall be responsible as a producer' (art. 3.2 of the Directive) – and thus jump over the hurdles, or chasms, devised by contract or business law. The Directive moreover incorporates

---

16   See A. Ojeda Avilés and L. Compa, 'Globalisation, class actions et droit du travail', in I. Daugareilh (ed.), *Mondialisation, travail et droits fondamentaux*, Brussels: Bruylant, 2005, 265–307.

17   European Directive 85/374, 25 July 1985.

incentives for tracing the product back to its producer, as formulated in article 3.3: 'Where the
producer of the product cannot be identified, each
supplier of the product shall be treated as its producer
unless he informs the injured person, within a reason-
able time, of the identity of the producer or of the
person who supplied him with the product.'[18]

So the idea that by following up a product's chain
of distribution and production one can assign liability at its source is beginning to be taken seriously in
contemporary law, as is the idea that it can best be
implemented through systems of product traceability.[19] Such a development signals the return of an old
medieval notion, that the product in some sense
remains imbued with the spirit of the person who
first put it into circulation, and who continues to be
liable for it despite changes of ownership. Feudal law
held that things are always received from another
(who could be God), such that one was never an
owner of a thing in the absolute sense of article 544
of the French Civil Code, but only its keeper.
Relations between people and things always preserved the imprint of relations between people.[20] As
Louis Dumont has shown, economic ideology implies
quite the reverse, that relations between people are
secondary to relations between people and things,[21]

18   Art. 3.3 of the Directive. The European Court of Justice has
reduced the scope of this principle of solidarity by condemning the way
the Directive was transposed into French law, where it allowed the
victim to sue the supplier, who could then, if so desired, sue the producer
(CJEC, case C-52/00 of 25 April 2002).
19   See M.-A. Hermitte, 'La traçabilité des personnes et des choses.
Précautions, pouvoirs et maîtrise', in Ph. Pédrot, *Traçabilité et
responsabilité*, Paris: Economica, 2003, 1ff.
20   See P. Ourliac and J. de Malafosse, *Histoire du droit privé*, vol. 2:
Les biens, Paris: PUF, 1971 (2nd ed.), 148ff.
21   L. Dumont, *From Mandeville to Marx: The Genesis and Triumph
of Economic Ideology*, Chicago: University of Chicago Press, 1983.

and since the market economy requires goods for exchange, these need to be stripped of any trace of personal bonds. The direct relation of people to things (treated in book II of the French Civil Code) became the basis of contractual relations between people (treated, along with successions, in book III). The case of dangerous objects, which has arisen due to technological advances, has obliged us to go back to an older conception and reinstate the idea that behind things there are people who are accountable for them.

The application of this idea that behind every thing there is a liable person remains confined, at the international level, to harm caused by defective products. It does not extend to the working conditions or the effects on the environment of the product's manufacture; the WTO considers that restrictions may apply to the free circulation of a product on the grounds of protecting people's health and security only if it is the product which is harmful and not its mode of production.[22] But there are strong arguments in favour of including the conditions of manufacture under this rule. The first argument is historical. This type of liability was first introduced into domestic law in the sphere of labour relations. Since the worker receives his or her work from the employer – both the thing to be worked on and the tools to be used, while having no rights over these – legislation on industrial injury makes the employer responsible for any damage caused by the work. At the end of the nineteenth century, identifying the person benefiting from a dangerous product was a way out of the difficulties

22   The General Agreement on Tariffs and Trade (GATT), art. XX, § b. R. Howse and D. Regan criticise this restrictive interpretation, 'The Product/Process Distinction – An Illusory Basis for Disciplining "Unilateralism" in Trade Policy', *European Journal of International Law* 11: 2, 2000, 249–89.

of liability based on fault, and ensured that someone could be held responsible for such injury. The second argument is legal. Law on international trade can only exclude the conditions under which goods are manufactured if these do not bear intangible elements such as trademarks, patents or rights to use, whose ownership is separate from the person in possession of the product. If the market value of a product derives for the most part from these intellectual property rights, then any policing agency is obliged to investigate whether these rights have been respected in the product's manufacture and transfer. Although there is no concrete difference between an original musical recording or software programme and its perfect copy, a country has the right and the duty to prohibit circulation of the latter. Since intellectual property is at the very heart of the 'new economy', it is vital for transnational companies to ensure that such copies cannot circulate freely, and hence that safeguarding property rights by inspecting conditions of product manufacture should take precedence over the imperative of free circulation.[23] This implies that intellectual property rights occupy the same structural position as social rights, as regards trade regulation: neither can be assimilated to the concrete possession of goods, and both require the positive intervention of states. And these rights can only be enforced if the product is traceable, since traceability alone guarantees that the product was manufactured lawfully.

The fact that the conditions of manufacture of a product must be scrutinised in the case of intellectual property rights, yet dismissed when it is a question of protecting fundamental workers' rights, is yet another example of how ends and means have come to be

---

23   See the TRIPS Agreement annexed to the Marrakesh Agreement establishing the WTO.

inverted under the total market. But this example at least has the merit of demonstrating that legal means do exist to impel transnational companies to assume responsibility for how their products are manufactured.

9

CIRCLES OF SOLIDARITY

The concept of solidarity, like many of our categories of thought, comes from Roman law. It served to offset the drawbacks of having a multiplicity of creditors (active solidarity) or of debtors (passive solidarity) for the same obligation: solidarity means that the presence of others does not diminish the responsibility of each.[1] Sociologists and political theorists of the late nineteenth century found in solidarity a satisfactory way of remedying the excesses of individualism without bringing back the old religious or corporatist insular communities of the pre-industrial era. The great advantage of solidarity was precisely that it grounded the techniques of social law in contract law, and so preserved the principles of equality and individual liberty, which any mention of 'natural communities' would have compromised. After being transplanted into social law, the notion of solidarity evolved and even became, in some countries, the only general principle on which the social security system was based.[2] This shift from

1 Justinian's *Digest*, 45, 2.2. See Ch. Demangeat, *Des obligations solidaires en droit romain*, Paris: A. Marescq, 1858.
2 See the first article of the French Social Security Code (art. L.111-1): 'The system of social security is founded on the principle of national solidarity.'

local solidarities based on membership of traditional communities to large solidarity systems controlled by the state characterises the history of systems of social protection, however varied they may be in other ways.[3]

Solidarity, as it is understood in social law, consists in establishing a common fund within a group of individuals to which all must contribute according to their capacities and upon which each may draw according to his or her needs. The obligation upon each to contribute to the protection of all is certainly a human duty, implicitly or explicitly affirmed in declarations of fundamental human rights. The pooling of resources implies outlawing the calculation of individual utility and replacing it with that of collective utility, which the solidarity system puts into practice. From an economic viewpoint, a common fund relies on an agreement to privilege the interests of members over those of third parties and the collective over the individual interest. The services within its remit are protected from free competition, and its members' individual freedom restricted. This is why, in a world where the legal realm is in thrall to market ideology, such systems can flourish and gain recognition only by establishing their own legal foundations. And since the principle of solidarity can provide just such a basis, it has gradually come to acquire the value of a legal principle in European Community law.[4] Solidarity embodies what is, after all, a very simple idea – that every human society needs both cooperation and competition. Any society which dismisses

3   See my 'Sur le principe de solidarité', *Zeitschrift des Max-Planck-Instituts für europäische Rechtsgeschichte* 6, 2005, 67–81.
4   CJEC, 17 Feb. 1993, Cases C-159 and 160/91 (Poucet and Pistre), *Droit Social* 1993, 488, note Ph. Laigre and obs. J.-J. Dupeyroux; CJEC, 16 Nov. 1995, Case C-244/94 (Coreva); CJEC, 26 March 1996, Case C-238/94 (Garcia). See J.-J. Dupeyroux, 'Les exigences de la solidarité', *Droit Social* 1990, 741.

either of these needs is doomed to failure, since the cooperative advantage is as determinant for a society's prosperity and well-being as its competitive advantage.

The recognition of the principle of solidarity in the legal field signals the reappearance of non-contractual forms of exchange. Every contract is based on the calculation of individual utility, and the freedom to contract is quite simply the freedom to be bound by nothing that does not further one's individual self-interest. The jurists who today attempt to absorb the concept of solidarity into contract law are labouring in vain. When, for example, contributory pension schemes are described as a 'contract between the generations', this is not simply wrong (since generations are not legal subjects capable of signing contracts, and those to come are already bound by the system before they even enter the world), but it also betrays a profound misrecognition of the real nature of these schemes. They derive from non-contractual forms of obligation and are still today a kind of response to what anthropologists call the 'debt of life'.[5] Anthropologically speaking, one receives life from the previous generation, gives it to the following one and, by giving it, repays the debt to the preceding generation. In terms of pension schemes, those who gave to the previous generation will receive from the following one – and thus, what is received from one generation is given back by another. Clearly the system makes no sense unless we take into account at least three consecutive generations. The right to a retirement pension and its corollary of the duty to make welfare contributions reintroduce elements which are incomprehensible to contract law, namely

---

5   See C. Malamoud, *Debt and Debtors*, New Delhi: Vikas Publishing, 1983, and the adage from the Brahmanic tradition: 'As soon as man is born, he is born in person as a debt owing to death' (30).

the time frame and the vertical axis of the succession of generations.

In light of the above, it should come as no surprise that we have Africa to thank for the first formal declaration of the principle of solidarity. When African jurists were enjoined to adopt the credo of Western human rights, they set about adapting them to their own culture and experience. The African Charter on Human and Peoples' Rights (1981) incorporates the individual rights which feature in Western declarations, but does so within a conception of the human being not as isolated individual subject, but as a being linked to others. Whereas in the Universal Declaration of 1948, the principle of solidarity is implicitly only conceived in terms of individual *rights* (rights to social security, to an adequate standard of living, to security in case of loss of one's means of subsistence: see art. 22 and art. 25), in the African Charter it is formulated as a *duty* (art. 29-4: 'The individual shall have the duty to preserve and strengthen social and national solidarity'). In the first case, solidarity takes the form of a claim on society, in the second, of a debt. In reality, however, rights and duties are always linked. The rights of Western systems have always been coupled with the duty to contribute to welfare schemes through compulsory contributions (taxes and social security contributions). This duty is explicitly formulated in the American Declaration of the Rights and Duties of Man (1948), which states that every person is obliged 'to cooperate with the state and the community with respect to social security and welfare, in accordance with his ability and with existing circumstances' (art. 35), and 'to pay the taxes established by law for the support of public services' (art. 36).

Twenty years after the African Declaration, the European Charter of Fundamental Rights adopted at Nice in 2000 endorsed in turn the principle of solidarity, while extending it further. The Charter includes under 'solidarity' (chap. IV, art. 27ff.) not only the social rights figuring in the Universal Declaration but also new fundamental rights (workers' rights to information, rights to collective bargaining and collective action, rights of access to public services) and certain principles that both public authorities and businesses must respect (ensuring compatibility between family and working life, and environmental and consumer protection). So the principle of solidarity has given rise to well-defined obligations, which are binding on easily identifiable legal subjects who can be sanctioned by law if these are not complied with. For example, the obligation to pay one's taxes, to contribute to funding the social security system, to consult employees, to protect the environment, to ensure that working hours are compatible with a normal family life, and so forth. Another innovative aspect of the principle of solidarity, as expressed in the Nice Charter, is that it provides a basis not only for rights to protection but also to the exercise of certain freedoms. This is true at the collective level – the principle of solidarity grounds the freedom to associate and the right to strike – but also for the individual, since the principle of harmonising working and family life opens up new possibilities of action for both women and men.

If solidarity, just like dignity, were given a minimum of serious attention, as a legal principle from which, inseparably, both rights and duties follow, we might be able to leave behind the sterile debates on the 'justiciability' of economic and social rights. To put it succinctly, any measures used by natural or legal persons to evade the duties deriving from the principle of solidarity infringe human rights, and the culprits should be brought to trial and sentenced as such. For example, when a company relocates, or subcontracts its production, solely with a view to evading the employment and environmental legislation governing the markets on which it sells its products. Or, a fortiori, when

international institutions like the World Bank pander
to the narrow interests of investors and infringe human
rights by encouraging competition between legal systems. If these sorts of violations of fundamental social
rights can occur on the part of the institutions which
supervise international trade, it is because solidarity is
a principle which was first developed in the legal framework of nation states, whereas institutions of this sort
are precisely bent on curbing the latter's scope of
action, beginning with the weakest. And solidarity systems are fundamentally anathema to these institutions,
since they differentiate between people along lines of
affiliation rather than wealth and do not obey the logic
of individual utility.

However, in criticising neo-liberal ideology, we
should not lose sight of the objective factors which
destabilise national social security systems. We no
longer live in a world which can be represented as a
mosaic of sovereign states that choose freely their relations to each other. The possibilities opened up,
particularly for communication, by the revolution in
technology, and also its attendant risks, have bound all
countries in the world into a network of objective solidarity. None may consider themselves to be immune to
the epidemics, poverty, environmental catastrophes,
fanaticism or violent outbursts that may plague their
neighbours. And all are faced with a disintegration of
the social bond whose increasing and already exorbi-
tant costs to social security systems will in the long
term prove unsustainable. Moreover, given the major
role that different forms of solidarity have always
played in civil society, the current destabilisation of
family and working life strikes at the very heart of
social security systems. These different developments
mean that the principle of solidarity at the basis of
social security can no longer be interpreted solely in
terms of national solidarity. It is not that the latter disappears, but rather that, whereas it previously played

an exclusive role, today it is a nexus to which other networks of solidarity, both intra- and inter-national, must be linked.

First, the relations between social security systems and the different forms of solidarity in civil society must be rethought. The development of social security has up to now accelerated rather than hindered the spread of individualism. Affiliation to anonymous institutions has helped free individuals from the work-related, familial or religious communities which were traditionally the matrix of solidarity. Financial resources, rather than personal bonds, have become the principle guarantee against risk (an aspect which is obscured by analyses of the welfare state in terms of 'decommodification').[6] It is significant in this respect that in certain African languages the word 'poor' does not mean what the World Bank means by it – an income of less than two dollars a day – but 'someone who has few people', that is, who has no one to count on for solidarity.[7] In this light, our societies of the rich are full of the poor, whose ranks have been swelled, paradoxically, by social security systems, and whose poverty no one ever dreams of measuring. Of course, good pensions and good health insurance enable the elderly not to be dependent on their offspring, which is unquestionably an advance. But these do not prevent isolation, which can be fatal, as the French heat wave of 2003 proved: older people who were economically poor but socially rich fared better than those in the opposite situation. More generally, no system of social security can cover the expenses arising from a society

6   G. Esping-Andersen, *The Three Worlds of Welfare Capitalism*, Princeton: Princeton University Press, 1990.
7   See J. Nguebou-Toukam and M. Fabre-Magnan, 'La tontine: une leçon africaine de solidarité', in *Du droit du travail aux droits de l'humanité. Études offertes à Philippe-Jean Hesse*, Rennes: Presses Universitaires de Rennes, 2003, 299ff.

composed entirely of solitary individuals, who have no one to count on in case of illness. In other words, our countries' national solidarity systems instituted by social security continue to rely on solidarity networks within society, and particularly on familial solidarity which, although restricted to a narrower circle of people, still plays a major role. Just as labour law should acknowledge the unpaid work done outside the sphere of the market, so social security legislation should not only acknowledge but actively support the different forms of solidarity in society. These two aspects are clearly linked, for example in provision for dependent elderly people, when it is necessary both to ensure that they can be looked after in their own homes and that the children involved do not jeopardise their jobs to do so.

There are two reasons why the much-needed valorisation of solidarity within civil society should be regarded today not as a means or a pretext for weakening national social security networks, but on the contrary for strengthening them. The first reason concerns the profound changes the welfare state has helped bring about. Extended families and solidarity within one's profession or parish are things of the past, and while we should support the living forms of solidarity in society, it is useless to want to resuscitate those which have already disappeared. The second reason is that national solidarity must continue to be a nexus for other systems. It cannot be repeated often enough that all institutions based on the principle of solidarity privilege the collective over the individual interest, and the interests of members of the group over those external to it. Only the state can ensure that these institutions serve the general interest and that the cost to individual freedom is not too high. And only the state can articulate the different solidarity structures which exist alongside the national system, be they work-related, community-based, or in the form of mutual insurance.

If these structures are not given a coherent national framework, society risks fragmenting into inward-looking groups on the one hand, and the mass of those belonging to no group on the other. This is why the realisation of the principle of solidarity in practice must remain the remit of the state. The state must respect the autonomy of other solidarity networks but also oblige them to contribute to national solidarity and to adhere to the other founding principles of social security – namely dignity, equality and access.

One of the first areas in which these sorts of reforms should be introduced is doubtless health coverage. The system is on the verge of bankruptcy in France, a fact which cannot be hidden much longer simply by carrying over payment of today's costs onto future generations.[8] The reasons why expenditure has spiralled out of control here are obviously complex. Contributing factors certainly include, to varying degrees, the ageing of the population, the increasing precariousness of living and working conditions, the constant advances in medical technology, and the abuse of an undiscerning system by unscrupulous patients and doctors. But one thing remains certain: no solutions to these problems will be forthcoming unless we rethink the relation between health professionals and the health insurance system. The latter is forced to cover costs over which it has no control, except for transferring them partly or wholly onto the patients

8 The French CADES (*Caisse d'amortissement de la dette sociale*), established in 1996, was nominated to oversee this deferral of payment. Its remit was to absorb the social security deficit (a sum of €21 billion at the time) by borrowing on the financial markets. It has in fact managed, unchecked, to dig an ever deeper hole in the social security budget. While the CADES should have been abolished in 2009, its mandate has been regularly renewed, and the French Parliament regularly entrusts it with dealing with ever vaster debts (for example, an additional €26.9 billion of social security deficits were transferred to it at the end of 2008, of which €14.1 billion were health insurance debts alone).

themselves. Its contracts with the medical unions are an outright failure, since the profession refuses any change to the fee-for-service principle or the freedom to set up a practice wherever one wishes. The medical profession fears, understandably, that it will be made hostage to a huge bureaucratic machine which understands nothing but figures. But the result of this impasse is, despite soaring expenditure, the tacit advance of a two-tier system, the appearance of geographical areas without doctors, a decline in general medicine, and a huge increase in the number of consultations charged above the statutory rate, as well as under-the-counter payments.

The vast and impersonal mechanisms of national solidarity still remain the most powerful, equitable and effective way of *financing* health coverage. However, despite the hopes placed in the democratic management of the institutions of national solidarity after the Second World War, the latter have proved incapable of managing health insurance *expenses* judiciously. Good management would mean forging relations of trust with doctors and patients, which requires smaller and less anonymous circles of solidarity – and certainly not a system which is by its very nature centralised and anonymous. In the French context, this role should be played by the mutual insurance societies. These non-profit organisations are sufficiently well established to have resisted the onslaught of the European Commission (which, unable to conceive of anything between the state and the market, has attempted to sacrifice them on the altar of its binary thinking). But today these societies have only an ancillary role, and no decision-making power in the running of the health system. The government devolves onto them the costs it wants to spare social security while refusing to reciprocate by giving them a say in how the money should be spent. Yet that is precisely what should be happening, because the mutual societies are the only institutions capable of making really binding agreements with health professionals, and they are much closer to this constituency than are the national institutions. Such agreements are vital to the goal of 'extending preventive medicine, guaranteeing equal access for all to the care each requires, ensuring continuity of care and the best health safeguards possible'.[9] Were mutual societies to play the role of interface between the health insurance system and health professionals, we could put a stop to some of the absurdities of the present system, notably the fee-for-service formula, which encourages doctors to see as many patients as possible, penalises those who still take the time to discuss with patients, and rewards those who replace a conversation with a battery of technical prescriptions. Mutual societies are best placed to respond to the profound sociological changes affecting the medical profession and to advocate methods of remuneration for health professionals which encourage appropriate care, valorise general medicine, support dialogue between doctor and patient (a lack of which translates into increased litigation), and ensure good territorial distribution of doctors' surgeries. Empowering institutions based on smaller circles of solidarity would strengthen rather than weaken national solidarity, on which the health insurance system must continue to rest. And this less spendthrift medicine would be able to be attentive to all the causes of human suffering, instead of gradually metamorphosing into a particularly ruinous practice of joiner-fitters.

Secondly, national social security systems can no longer ignore that today's risks are global, and consequently that solidarity mechanisms must be developed on an international scale. Among the many factors which make it futile to simply turn inwards to the sphere of national solidarity are the epidemics and pathogenic agents which can spread rapidly and

9   Public Health Code, art. L, 1110-1.

unchecked across the globe, the increase in ecological risks on a global scale, the ageing of the population in 'rich' countries, and the mass emigration of populations fleeing the insecurity and poverty rife in many Southern countries. If we respond to these types of risk by clinging to the sphere of national solidarity alone, we will find ourselves imprisoned in an aporetic logic that is perfectly exemplified by the debate on the welfare status of illegal immigrants: short of revoking the fundamental social rights which figure in our most important founding texts, we cannot deny someone the right, which is integral to his or her dignity as a human being, to social security; at the same time, however, we cannot extend solidarity to every inhabitant of the planet who is deprived of this right. So far, we have tried to overcome this aporia in two ways. We have broadened access to social benefits by changing the criteria so that some or all of the illegal immigrants residing in the country for a certain length of time become eligible, and we have erected Maginot Lines supposed to protect Europe from a mass influx of illegal immigrants. These strategies are neither adequate nor sustainable in the long run. They transform access to fundamental social rights into the prize for which thousands of individuals daily embark on death-defying journeys to scale the fortress into which we have retreated. Those who die along the way, who are turned back or who try to survive one way or another in their home country remain excluded from the circle of national solidarity and abandoned to their fate.

We will not be able to resolve these aporias while social security continues to be conceived as a set of self-enclosed national systems of solidarity, divorced from the economic realm. A problem such as mass illegal immigration cannot be adequately addressed unless we examine its causes, particularly the injustice of the international trade regime, and unless we focus on its effects, not only in the countries of immigration but also of emigration. What impels young Africans to risk their lives in emigrating to Europe is the destitution and economic insecurity of their home countries after twenty years of structural adjustment programmes and trade deregulation, and the absence of decent work. Showing solidarity with illegal immigrants is certainly necessary, but if the goal is for fundamental social rights to be respected everywhere, it is a subsidiary aspect. Our core task is to transform the negative solidarity which dominates inter-state relations today into a positive solidarity based on common objectives of decent work and just treatment in the trade arrangements between countries. The principle of solidarity must be placed at the very heart of any international trade regulations (which would imply, notably, ensuring 'stability in world prices of primary products': DePh, art. IV). And measures for evaluating such regulation in terms of its real effects on people's economic security must be introduced (DePh, art. IIc). Intra-European relations should also be based on solidarity. It is not too late to call a halt to competition between social protection and fiscal regimes within the EU, which inflames nationalistic and protectionist sentiments. Bismarck was perspicacious enough to use the fledgling social insurance of his time to cement German unity at the end of the nineteenth century. Why should Europe not be capable of developing instruments of solidarity designed to support the capacities of its workers at the beginning of the twenty-first? Europe could well set the example and work to reinstate the hierarchy of ends and means which the Declaration of Philadelphia has already enshrined.

APPENDIX: THE DECLARATION OF PHILADELPHIA, 10 MAY 1944

The declaration concerning the aims and purposes of the International Labour Organisation, here reprinted, was unanimously adopted by the International Labour Conference at its twenty-sixth session, held at Philadelphia, from 20 April to 12 May 1944.

The text of the declaration as here presented is a true copy of the text authenticated by the signatures of the president of the International Labour Conference and of the acting director of the International Labour Office.

DECLARATION CONCERNING THE AIMS AND PURPOSES OF THE INTERNATIONAL LABOUR ORGANISATION

The General Conference of the International Labour Organisation, meeting in its Twenty-sixth Session in Philadelphia, hereby adopts, this tenth day of May in the year nineteen hundred and forty-four, the present Declaration of the aims and purposes of the International Labour Organisation and of the principles which should inspire the policy of its Members.

I

The Conference reaffirms the fundamental principles on which the Organisation is based and, in particular, that:

(a) labour is not a commodity;

(b) freedom of expression and of association are essential to sustained progress;

(c) poverty anywhere constitutes a danger to prosperity everywhere;

(d) the war against want requires to be carried on with unrelenting vigour within each nation, and by continuous and concerted international effort in which the representatives of workers and employers, enjoying equal status with those of Governments, join with them in free discussion and democratic decision with a view to the promotion of the common welfare.

II

Believing that experience has fully demonstrated the truth of the statement in the Constitution of the International Labour Organisation that lasting peace can be established only if it is based on social justice, the Conference affirms that:

(a) all human beings, irrespective of race, creed or sex, have the right to pursue both their material well-being and their spiritual development in conditions of freedom and dignity, of economic security and equal opportunity;

(b) the attainment of the conditions in which this shall be possible must constitute the central aim of national and international policy;

(c) all national and international policies and measures, in particular those of an economic and financial character, should be judged in this light and accepted only in so far as they may be held to promote and not to hinder the achievement of this fundamental objective;

(d) it is a responsibility of the International Labour Organisation to examine and consider all international economic and financial policies and measures in the light of this fundamental objective;

(e) in discharging the tasks entrusted to it the International Labour Organisation, having considered all relevant economic and financial factors, may include in its decisions and recommendations any provisions which it considers appropriate.

III

The Conference recognises the solemn obligation of the International Labour Organisation to further among the nations of the world programmes which will achieve:

(a) full employment and the raising of standards of living;

(b) the employment of workers in the occupations in which they can have the satisfaction of giving the fullest measure of their skill and attainments and make their greatest contribution to the common well-being;

(c) the provision, as a means to the attainment of this end and under adequate guarantees for all concerned, of facilities for training and the transfer of labour, including migration for employment and settlement;

(d) policies in regard to wages and earnings, hours and other conditions of work calculated to ensure a just share of the fruits of progress to all, and a minimum living wage to all employed and in need of such protection;

(e) the effective recognition of the right of collective bargaining, the co-operation of management and labour in the continuous improvement of productive efficiency, and the collaboration of workers and employers in the preparation and application of social and economic measures;

(f) the extension of social security measures to provide a basic income to all in need of such protection and comprehensive medical care;

(g) adequate protection for the life and health of workers in all occupations;

(h) provision for child welfare and maternity protection;

(i) the provision of adequate nutrition, housing and facilities for recreation and culture;

(j) the assurance of equality of educational and vocational opportunity.

IV

Confident that the fuller and broader utilisation of the world's productive resources necessary for the achievement of the objectives set forth in this Declaration can be secured by effective international and national action, including measures to expand production and consumption, to avoid severe economic fluctuations, to promote the economic and social advancement of the less developed regions of the world, to assure greater stability in world prices of primary products, and to promote a high and steady volume of international trade, the Conference pledges the full co-operation of the International Labour Organisation with such international bodies as may be entrusted with a share of the responsibility for this great task and for the promotion of the health, education and well-being of all peoples.

V

The Conference affirms that the principles set forth in this Declaration are fully applicable to all peoples everywhere and that, while the manner of their application must be determined with due regard to the stage of social and economic development reached by each people, their progressive application to peoples who are still dependent, as well as to those who have already achieved self-government, is a matter of concern to the whole civilised world.

The foregoing is the authentic text of the Declaration concerning the aims and purposes of the International Labour Organisation unanimously adopted by the General Conference of the International Labour Organisation at Philadelphia during its Twenty-Sixth Session, on 10 May 1944.

IN FAITH WHEREOF we have appended our signatures, this seventeenth day of May 1944.

The President of the Conference, W. NASH

The Acting Director of the International Labour Office, EDWARD J. PHELAN